THRIVE²

LIVING AND LEADING A WIN-WIN-WIN ORGANIZATIONAL CULTURE

DR. JANICE MCLAUGHLIN GEORGE

outskirts press

THRIVE²
Living and Leading a Win-Win-Win Organizational Culture
All Rights Reserved.
Copyright © 2021 Dr. Janice McLaughlin George
v6.0

The opinions expressed in this manuscript are solely the opinions of the author and do not represent the opinions or thoughts of the publisher. The author has represented and warranted full ownership and/or legal right to publish all the materials in this book.

This book may not be reproduced, transmitted, or stored in whole or in part by any means, including graphic, electronic, or mechanical without the express written consent of the publisher except in the case of brief quotations embodied in critical articles and reviews.

Outskirts Press, Inc.
http://www.outskirtspress.com

Paperback ISBN: 978-1-9772-2695-2
Hardback ISBN: 978-1-9772-2735-5

Cover Photo © 2021 www.gettyimages.com. All rights reserved - used with permission.

Outskirts Press and the "OP" logo are trademarks belonging to Outskirts Press, Inc.

PRINTED IN THE UNITED STATES OF AMERICA

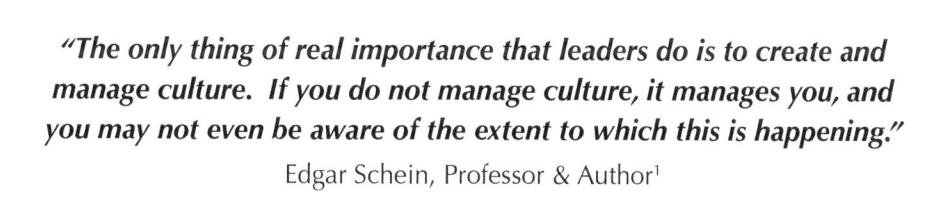

"The only thing of real importance that leaders do is to create and manage culture. If you do not manage culture, it manages you, and you may not even be aware of the extent to which this is happening."

Edgar Schein, Professor & Author[1]

Table of Contents

Foreword i
Preface iii
Acknowledgements v
Chapter 1: Introduction - Why THRIVE²! 1
Part 1: Who We Are (Our Character) 9
    Chapter 2: Trust - The Foundation for a Thriving Culture 11
    Chapter 3: Health for a Thriving Culture 19
    Chapter 4: Respect from the Heart to Thrive 29
    Chapter 5: Image that Thrives 43
    Chapter 6: Values that Thrive 53
    Chapter 7: Ethics that Thrive 67
Part 2: What We Do (Our Performance) 77
    Chapter 8: Teamwork that Thrives 79
    Chapter 9: Holism with Continuous Learning to Thrive 89
    Chapter 10: Responsibility that Thrives with Results 101
    Chapter 11: Innovation with Intentional Care that Thrives 111
    Chapter 12: Vision with Strategic Execution that Thrives 121
    Chapter 13: Empowerment to Thrive 129
    Chapter 14: Now THRIVE²! 139
Endnotes 149
References 173

Foreword

DURING MY 30-PLUS years of working in corporate America and my five years as a business owner, I have been privileged to serve in leadership positions, as I have done for more than half of those years. Some of that time, I had the opportunity to be in the presence of some of the country's best and brightest leaders as they led profitable organizations in the transportation, telecommunications, and financial services industries. Throughout my career, I have also encountered leaders who were challenged to exhibit leadership expertise but did not possess the competencies required for an organization to thrive. The latter group of leaders was not leading, only taking a walk, because they were ineffective and had no one following their flawed leadership models. Because of this, both their companies and their employees suffered.

However, in my quest to become a strong leader, one who people would want to follow, I modeled my behavior after exemplary leaders in the community, within both my organization and other leading companies—people who led not only with their intellect but also with their hearts. Those leaders helped shape my leadership acumen and my successful career as an executive leading cultural transformation in Fortune 100 companies such as US Airways, Verizon Communications, Freddie Mac, and Fannie Mae. Leading in these organizations has afforded me opportunities to speak across the United States and internationally on courageous leadership and leading through culture change. As the only person to have served as vice president and chief diversity and inclusion officer at both Freddie Mac and Fannie Mae, I am humbled to receive various recognition from such publications as *Savoy Magazine* ("Top 100 Executives in America"), *Profiles in Diversity* ("Women Worth Watching"), *Black Enterprise* ("Top Fifty Chief Diversity Officers"), *Working Mother Magazine* ("Working Mother of the Year"), and *Washington Business Journal*. Although leadership is recognized, the success of a leader is about leveraging others' capabilities for advancement.

When my esteemed colleague and longtime dear friend shared with me that her second book would be about leadership, I was excited and could not wait for the release. You see, Dr. George is a leader's leader who is committed to leading others! She shows her leadership skills not just in the workplace but also in her community and in her church. I had the privilege to serve with her as she led the Antioch Baptist Church women's ministry. Dr. George is a woman of strong character, and she leads from her core of integrity and respect for all. Her servant's heart is equal to her intellect as she establishes her vision and drives toward productivity and profitability. She elicits the desire in her followers to excel and do their best work.

In *THRIVE²: Living and Leading a Win-Win-Win Organizational Culture,* Dr. George has created a handbook for the reader who desires to create a win-win-win culture in his or her workplace. That workplace can be in the community, a Fortune 500 company, a government agency, a nonprofit organization, or a small business. *THRIVE²: Living and Leading a Win-Win-Win Organizational Culture* is relevant to anyone who wants to establish a healthy, inclusive, and thriving culture focused on the betterment of their organization.

If you are committed to continuous improvement and leading or working in an environment comprised of stellar leaders with strong character, integrity, and courage, then *THRIVE²: Living and Leading a Win-Win-Win Organizational Culture* is the book for you. If you are committed to creating an organization that is value-driven, with trust, respect, and work-life balance, and where ethics abound, this is the book for you.

This playbook is full of examples of competencies and challenges for you to assess your leadership style, and each chapter ends with a checklist to evaluate your current environment. The author also provides a "to-do" list to help you reach the pinnacle of strong leadership. Dr. George provides you with the what, the why, and the how of THRIVE by ACT: Assess Your Attitude and Actions, Commit to Personal and Organizational Changes, and Transform Your Thoughts. All that is left for you, the reader, is to ACT to THRIVE!

Tujuanna B. Williams
Founder & CEO, Tujuanna Williams Consulting, LLC
Former VP and Chief Diversity & Inclusion Officer, Freddie Mac & Fannie Mae

Preface

ORGANIZATIONAL CULTURE, WHETHER in the workplace, community establishments, churches, academic institutions, or even the home, has always fascinated me. I enjoy observing and assessing leaders, followers, their interactions, and people in general, including my own experiences, from job interviews (virtual and in-person) to becoming an employee and experiencing the organization's culture. In a Fortune 100 organization, I also had the privilege to be a culture assessor, working with a team of people to evaluate various departments within the organization on their commitment to and execution of the company's cultural principles. In essence, culture has been an integral part of my life, and I recognize its snowball effect on the success of organizations and employees in all areas of life, including career, health, personal goals, family, and other relationships.

My passion for culture was further ignited during my doctoral studies in strategic leadership, which led to the writing of this book. As I completed the program, I needed to decide on a final project. I knew I wanted to write a manuscript, but I struggled to choose a topic—the leadership skills needed in the workplace or the make-up of a winning culture, both of which are dear to my heart. My challenge was that both of them are interdependent—leaders impact culture, and they need the right cultural environment to be effective (i.e., this is a chicken-or-egg-first situation). Leadership and culture go hand in hand.

When the time came to make the final decision and submit my proposal, I decided it was best to lay out the vision and foundation of a healthy culture wherein everyone thrives. Choosing this topic enabled me to summarize my learning meaningfully with the end goal of equipping leaders and employees at all levels. Although the focus of this book is definitely on the workplace, one can apply these concepts to every team or organization one belongs to, including in the home—with family and friends.

Even though every person in the organization influences the culture, leaders have the primary responsibility to live, lead, and promote the desired culture, and they have the position of authority to affect the necessary changes. Therefore, I wrote this book to help leaders formulate and articulate a vision and the ingredients necessary to create the ideal culture and assess their individual impact on culture. For employees who also contribute to their organization's culture, this book provides a tool to guide their actions and influence on culture and assess culture as they make career decisions. To develop and maintain this desired culture, everyone has to understand that the process takes time and patience. The transformation occurs one person or team at a time, beginning with the persons in the mirror—you and me.

When I wrote my first book, *Confident Love*, I wrote the content first and then struggled to determine the right title. This time, I had the opposite experience. Once I settled on the topic, organizational culture, the word, "thrive," became my focus, serving not only as the book's title but also as its purpose, to enable the organization and everyone to thrive.

Because I enjoy writing in an acrostic fashion to help the reader remember the concepts and allow me to be creative and have fun, the title of this book, Thrive, became THRIVE^2, in which each letter addresses the needed character (the who) and performance (the what) of a thriving organization. In other words, the book addresses the factors to THRIVE in character and THRIVE in performance. Each chapter encourages the reader to ACT—assess attitude and actions, commit to personal and organizational changes, and transform one's thoughts. The section for transforming thoughts includes at least three associated quotes to inspire the reader on the journey; however, in some chapters, I had difficulty choosing, so I included a lot more.

I am excited about this book and the positive impact it will have on you and the organization and people you serve while you work together to achieve individual and corporate goals. As you spend most of your days at work, may you wake up with a smile on your face and pep in your step, looking forward to work—looking forward to thriving in every area of your life. May you have a rewarding, life-changing influence on your team, organization, community, nation, and world!

Thank you for embarking on this journey with me.

May you be blessed as you THRIVE^2 to win!

Dr. Janice McLaughlin George
Founder & CEO, Leadership Passport
www.leadershippassport.com

Acknowledgements

I FIRST GIVE thanks to God, my heavenly Father, who gave me the vision to pursue my doctoral studies in strategic leadership at Regent University. I thank Him for giving me the courage, confidence and perseverance to continue the journey that led to the vision and creativity to write this book.

I thank my husband and best friend, Tom George, for his love, prayers, and support throughout the journey, making life easy for me to reach my goals.

I thank my mom, Verlena McLaughlin, who undergirds me and all my family with her prayers and encouragement. She laid the foundation that guided us from childhood to adulthood, ensuring that we had the tools and environment to perform well academically and all areas of life. If dad was here, I can see him smiling from ear to ear.

I thank the host of family, friends, and colleagues who supported me on this journey, attending workshops or focus groups, being the subjects of my projects, or giving me referrals. They continue to be a blessing in my life.

I thank Dr. Diane Wiater, my project chair and one of my favorite professors. I appreciate her coaching and encouraging me throughout this project (i.e., the writing of this book) and doctoral program. I also appreciate Dr. Virginia Richardson, another favorite professor, who was part of the review and approval process.

Many thanks to Dr. Doris Gomez and Dr. Kathleen Patterson for their vision in leading an excellent doctoral program that equips students and graduates with the leadership knowledge and practical application for the workplace.

I thank my friend and classmate, Dr. Adrienne Powell Ruffin, for embarking on this journey with me as we studied and prayed our way through and across the finish line together.

I thank my friend and role model, Tujuanna Brown Williams, for her sisterly friendship, support and encouragement along life's journey. I appreciate her taking the time to read the book and write the foreword.

I thank Dr. Marshal L. Ausberry, Sr., my pastor, for his input and consistently imparting wisdom to me in every area of life.

I thank Edward Prater for his expertise, enthusiasm about culture, and detailed feedback.

I thank the editors, Sharon Elliott and Laura Handley, for their sharp minds, thorough reviews and revisions.

I thank the entire Outskirts Press staff for helping me get this book on the shelf.

It takes a village to birth a book; I am thankful for the one God gave me. May God bless each of them.

CHAPTER 1

Introduction - Why THRIVE²!

"The culture of a workplace—an organization's values, norms, and practices— has a huge impact on our happiness and success."
ADAM GRANT, AUTHOR[1]

WENDY HAD RECEIVED several Starbucks gift cards but had never stepped foot in the coffee shop because she did not like coffee or understand all the hype about it. However, intrigued one spring Sunday morning with a book in hand, she redeemed one of the gift cards. Not knowing what to order, she walked up to the counter, told the cashier her story, and asked for suggestions. The cashier recommended a cinnamon dolce latte with a cinnamon swirl coffee cake. Wendy got her snack, found a nice cozy chair by a window, and made herself comfortable. She enjoyed her tasty treat, people watched, and read her book. Everything was terrific, and there was something uniquely appealing about the atmosphere, causing her to keep going back. She went back not just to redeem more gift cards, but because she enjoyed such a pleasant experience, interacting with some regulars who stopped by after a jog or church, or college students just waking up. Wendy was hooked!

When visiting Seattle, Washington on a business trip, adding some extra leisure time, Wendy also had the pleasure of touring Pike Place Market, the home of Starbucks. She bought coffee to share with family and friends when they visit her home and continues to bless others with Starbucks gift cards because she understands and appreciates the value of the experience and wants to gift it to others.

Over the years as she has learned more about Howard Schultz, Starbucks' second owner who transformed it into what it is today, Wendy has a better understanding and appreciation for Starbucks' success. Starbucks has leaders who care, and with this care, they created a culture with a meaningful purpose, yielding a great product, great service, and excellent results.

Howard Schultz demonstrates how having a meaningful purpose creates a successful company as Starbucks is "living proof that a company can lead with its heart and nurture its soul and still make money."[2] Being a person of humble beginnings, living in the projects of New York, and watching his dad suffer from a job-related injury with no workers' compensation, Mr. Schultz vowed that if ever he had the chance, he would make a difference in people's lives.[3] And what a difference he has made!

His vision of seeing Starbucks beyond its present enabled him to convince other investors of his vision, purchase the company and become CEO in 1987. He not only wanted customers to have a unique coffee experience of "warmth and community,"[4] he also wanted employees to have a unique work experience and compensation different from the hardships experienced by his dad. He wanted employees to be partners. He had a passion born from pain and created an environment wherein all personnel at all levels were treated with trust and respect. He had a heart that made a difference. He believed "if [a person] pours [his] heart into [his] work, or into any worthy enterprise, [he] can achieve dreams others may think impossible."[5]

Like Mr. Schultz, leaders have to have a vision and passion beyond making money to succeed. They have to answer their "why?"[6] The "why" determines the "what" and the "how." This "what"—a product, service, process, or experience—is whatever brings value to people, potential customers, and everything associated with it to enhance their experience.[7] Accordingly, leaders must ensure employees perform every action with excellence, understanding who the customer is and what the customer wants. Leaders also go the extra mile with no room for complacency to ensure quality, which can become a differentiator and yield a higher return on investment.[8] For this reason, leaders must build a culture wherein the organization acknowledges and values the diverse skills and talents of the employees, and everyone works together for the good of the company, teams, employees, customers, and communities.

When leaders have this right focus, they yield results and exceptional evaluations from everyone who matters. Employees are happy they work for leaders who take responsibility for the welfare of the people who run the day-to-day business.[9] Shareholders are delighted as they trust decisions are being made for the highest yield of return and enabling creativity and innovation to generate wealth.[10] The customers are also satisfied with the products and services, trusting the brand, and contributing to the word-of-mouth marketing.

On this journey to success, mistakes will happen, and challenges will come.[11] However, the leaders think positively and move forward, similar to the manner in which Howard Schultz did, not allowing the past, any failures, or naysayers to hinder his dreams of a brighter future for himself, the organization, and the people he serves. Leaders can let their challenges fuel their passion and commitment to making a difference, helping others along the way. In the words of Mr. Schultz, "because not everyone can take charge of his or her destiny, those who do rise to positions of authority have a responsibility... not only to steer the correct course but to make sure no one is left behind."[12]

Starbucks has a thriving culture. The people (i.e., the employees and customers) resonate with the culture—what Starbucks stands for.[13] "It's more than great coffee. It's the romance of the coffee experience, the feeling of warmth and community people get in Starbucks stores." This feeling, this atmosphere, is generated by the cashiers and baristas—the employees who take orders and create the made-to-order drinks for the customers. These employees not only know their product, but they also know they work for leaders who they trust and who have created a win-win-win culture where confidence, care, and respect reign.[14]

Any leader and organization who make people and culture a priority can thrive, and they can leverage this book for a visual and framework for what a thriving culture looks like. This book can help leaders create, live, and lead a win-win-win culture wherein organizations achieve their goals and delight customers and shareholders while employees achieve their career goals and enjoy their work, contributing to the betterment of the organization, community and world-at-large. In essence, this thriving culture can enable a win for the organization, a win for the employees, and a win for the customers. So what is organizational culture? Organizational culture is:

- A pattern of shared basic assumptions learned by a group as it solved its problems of external adaptation and internal integration, which has worked well enough to be considered valid and, therefore, to be taught to new members as the correct way to perceive, think, and feel in relation to those problems. *Organizational Culture and Leadership*[15]
- A corporate culture is the combination of the values and characteristics that define an organization. It influences the way employees relate to one another, to customers, to shareholders, and to business partners. It drives behaviors and unites employees around a shared set of values. It can lift [the] performance and improve [the] work environment. *The Future of Resource Management*[16]

Organizational culture is a consolidation of its values, preeminent leadership styles, success measures, processes and procedures, and means of communicating—words and symbols.[17] Some may simplify it by defining culture as "how we do things around here" and "how we think and feel about 'what we're doing here.'"[18] Culture is a powerful, competitive differentiator and can determine if an organization realizes its goals.[19]

Culture is the organization's personality.[20] It determines who wants to work for the company and how the people interact with each other. "The right culture can be the oil that makes the organization's internal mechanism work more smoothly and seamlessly. The wrong culture can act like sand in the oil, causing disruption and uneven or failing performance."[21] It can enable a positive brand, influencing employees, customers, and investors. Essentially, the corporate culture is a significant strategic asset, enabling the organization to achieve the following benefits:[22]

1. Organizational performance and success - Besides Starbucks, organizations like Google and Walmart attribute their success to culture.
   - Google is renowned for its work culture and is one of the best places to work; consequently, it attracts creative and technical personnel.[23] Their culture was an important asset at the beginning of the organization as they based their culture on three core values: "Don't be evil. Technology matters. We make our own rules."
   - The "Wal-Mart Way" is about how they treat their people and customers based on one of their core value statements: "We treat everyone with respect and dignity. We are in business to satisfy our customers. We strive for excellence in all we do."[24]
2. Strategic asset and consistent competitive advantage - Culture is the success factor that can be difficult and perhaps impossible to duplicate.[25]
3. Organizational stability - Culture creates an organizational glue, the mutual purpose and goals, with all employees marching to the same drummer despite their functional division and need to focus on achieving their specific missions. They all know they are contributing to the success of the corporate team.[26]
4. Successful partnerships - The success of mergers and acquisitions also depends on the cultural fit of all parties.
5. Financial and organizational performance - There is a proven relationship between culture and economic success.[27]
   - John Kotter and James Heskett completed a study of 207 U.S. companies and 22 industries, showing there is a positive relationship between culture and long-term financial performance.[28]
   - Eric Flamholtz conducted a survey, showing that up to 46% of EBIT (earnings before interest and taxes) was attributed to a positive culture.
   - Profits are higher when there is alignment between personal and organizational values. Employees are happy about being able to do what they enjoy and are good at, which aligns with the corporate mission. They do well when they know people value their opinions, and the team is committed to quality.[29]
   - While employees may have the skill and experience to succeed, there has to

be a cultural fit for overall success. For example, Carly Fiorina did not fit in with HP[30] and they eventually ended the relationship.
- Companies with a strong culture outperformed companies without a strong culture by a factor of six (6) and the stock market by a factor of 15. Also, earning profits was not the primary focus but a byproduct of a healthy culture.
- Culture is one of the six elements impacting organizational and financial success.[31] The other five factors include markets, resources, products and services, operational systems, and management systems. Culture is a crucial ingredient to success; without it, the other initiatives fail.[32]

Organizations and people thrive with the right culture. The leaders and founders of organizations set the culture and tone of the organization based on their personal and professional values, and the culture is then dissimilated to other team members through interactions, and informal means as employees imitate their leaders.[33] Therefore, it behooves leaders to determine the culture as soon as possible and to live and lead the preferred win-win-win culture. To this end, this book provides a vision and framework of a thriving culture. As there are two elements of culture—character and behavior (or performance), there are two primary parts to this book, THRIVE²:

Part 1 - Who We Are (Our Character)	
T	**Trust** - The Foundation for a Thriving Culture
H	**Health** for a Thriving Culture
R	**Respect** from the Heart to Thrive
I	**Image** that Thrives
V	**Values** that Thrive
E	**Ethics** that Thrive
Part 2 - What We Do (Our Performance)	
T	**Teamwork** that Thrives
H	**Holism** with Continuous Learning to Thrive
R	**Responsibility** that Thrives with Results
I	**Innovation** with Intentional Care that Thrives
V	**Vision** with Strategic Execution that Thrives
E	**Empowerment** to Thrive

Each chapter provides the vision and framework for the culture with practical application. As each chapter or topic could be a self-contained book, each chapter is by no means comprehensive but will help the reader visualize a culture that thrives and determine areas of improvement. Real stories are provided to demonstrate the cultural components discussed. Names, gender, industry, or other elements of the stories have been changed to maintain anonymity while keeping the integrity of the message. As the desired culture will not just happen, leaders have to be intentional and courageous to achieve a thriving work environment; therefore, each chapter encourages the reader to ACT (Assess, Commit, and Transform):

- Assess attitude and actions
- Commit to personal and organizational changes
- Transform thoughts

While the book is targeted at leaders who have the position, authority, and responsibility for the organizational culture and change management, all persons reading this book can make a difference by taking personal accountability for their attitude and actions and becoming a model for others to follow. The content and activities will equip the reader with information to have a positive influence on others if applied regardless of role, title or location (e.g., work or home). One's individual impact is not dependent on what others do although the effort will be enhanced by participation from others. Whether solo, a team, or entire organization, enjoy the journey to THRIVE², living and leading a win-win-win culture that makes a difference.

Conclusion

Culture is an essential element in the success of any organization. An organization can have a great vision, mission, strategy, and even great goals; however, without a strong, defined culture, all efforts are doomed.[34] The right culture will enable the organization to thrive. An unhealthy culture will be costly, resulting in lower employee satisfaction, higher turnover, lower profits, limited innovation, and unhappy customers and shareholders. The solution is simple—create a culture where leaders and employees have a shared vision, treat people right, and do the right thing while achieving goals that thrive.

Chapter 1 - THRIVE² ACT

Assess Your Attitude & Actions

Based on the content of this chapter, please assess your attitude and actions that influence the organization to THRIVE².

Chapter 1 Assessment	1	2	3	4	5
Rating Scale: 1=Strongly Disagree 2=Disagree 3=Neutral 4=Agree 5=Strongly Agree					
My organization understands, values and promotes a thriving culture.					
I understand, value and promote a thriving culture.					
I help my staff, peers, superiors, and stakeholders understand, value and promote a thriving culture.					

Commit to Personal & Organizational Changes

Based on what you know and have read regarding the significance of a thriving culture and your personal assessment above, what are you committing to improve for yourself, your staff, peers, superiors, stakeholders, or others?

Commitment	Commitment Date	Target Date
1.		
2.		
3.		

Transform Your Thoughts

"When it comes to landing a good job, many people focus on the role. Although finding the right title, position, and salary is important, there's another consideration that matters just as much: culture."
Adam Grant, Author[35]

"In determining the right people, the good-to-great companies placed greater weight on character attributes than on specific educational background, practical skills, specialized knowledge, or work experience."
Jim Collins, Business Consultant and Author[36]

"We can change culture if we change behavior."
Dr. Aubrey Daniels, Founder of ADI

"Always treat your employees exactly as you want them to treat your best customers."
Stephen R. Covey, Businessman and Author

"Culture guides discretionary behavior and it picks up where the employee handbook leaves off. Culture tells us how to respond to an unprecedented service request. It tells us whether to risk telling our bosses about our new ideas, and whether to surface or hide problems. Employees make hundreds of decisions on their own every day, and culture is our guide. Culture tells us what to do when the CEO isn't in the room, which is of course most of the time."
Frances Frei and Anne Morriss, Authors

Leaders ACT to THRIVE!

Part 1
Who We Are (Our Character)

Who We Are (Our Character)	
T	**Trust** - The Foundation for a Thriving Culture
H	**Health** for a Thriving Culture
R	**Respect** from the Heart to Thrive
I	**Image** that Thrives
V	**Values** that Thrive
E	**Ethics** that Thrive

CHAPTER **2**

Trust - The Foundation for a Thriving Culture

"Trust is the lubrication that makes it possible for organizations to work."
WARREN BENNIS, AUTHOR[1]

IN THE AFTERMATH of the 2001 US recession, a software development firm went through some major restructuring, including downsizing. There were literally changes every six months for at least a six-year period, ultimately cutting staff to almost half. Significant changes! Mary, like other leaders, struggled to keep up with the workload with the decreasing staff. While there was the formalized process of establishing individual and team goals, linking them at every level, during the restructuring, there was no time to revise goals and objectives formally as the organization evolved. There were even times when Mary and her team had to regroup weekly to determine the most important priorities for that week.

She experienced even greater challenges during software releases, managing all the marketing details, including equipping the sales teams for success. The manager and team combatted this problem and enabled success as they openly shared their views, strengths, and challenges so they could efficiently divide and conquer to meet deadlines with excellence. The team achieved their goals and thrived not only because of their commitment to excellence but because the team was founded on trust. The leader trusted her employees, and the team members trusted their leader and each other. They developed this trust before the storm, allowing them to work well together and achieve results during the storm.

Leaders, like Mary, are constantly bombarded with challenges. They address and adjust to the challenges in the marketplace and determine efficient, innovative ways to accomplish goals with internal and external partners.[2] Leaders have to change the "I" to "we" to work towards mutual goals, which requires mutual trust. They cannot succeed as leaders without trust. They need to trust their team to delegate responsibilities confidently to them; otherwise, they become micromanagers or a one-man team wherein no one wins. The team also needs to trust their leaders in order to achieve personal and corporate goals. So what is trust? *The Oxford Dictionary of Philosophy* defines trust as:

> The attitude of expecting good performance from another party, whether in terms of loyalty, goodwill, truth, or promises. The importance of trust as a kind of invisible glue binding people together is most visible when it is lost. Trust involves an element of risk, and epistemologists can have trouble categorizing it as rational, since it works best in advance, for example to motivate performance on occasions when defection may be to the advantage of the person trusted. Economically trust is precious, enabling parties to bypass the costly precautions and safeguards needed in transactions with parties whom one does not trust. Trustworthiness is a virtue, subsuming varieties such as truthfulness and fidelity. It is a general ambition of democratic politicians to be trusted whether or not they are trustworthy.[3]

Trust does not just happen.[4] It takes work, time, experiences, and consistency. There is a logical and technical component of trusting a person's competence, and an emotional element that enables connection through caring for others and their interests. Trust is the most significant quality employees use to assess their leaders.[5] Trust determines the degree to which employees will be vulnerable to their leaders' actions and behaviors.[6]

Trust is the oil that keeps relationships flowing.[7] When trust has not been achieved, or there is mistrust, relationships and performance suffer. Insecurities and levels of stress are demonstrated by people self-protecting themselves to minimize the risk of being misused. Mistrust may cause people to question another's motives. Cooperation, communication, and performance efficiencies are limited as employees use their time and energy to fight for their personal interests and goals. They are also not open to sharing new ideas, showing concern, or admitting their mistakes.[8] These challenges demonstrate that culture without trust is costly; therefore, leaders have to make every effort to build trust in the organization by understanding:

- Benefits of Trust
- Where Trust Begins
- Leadership Qualities for Building Trust
- How to Build and Maintain Trust

Benefits of Trust

Organizations with high levels of trust are more profitable than those with low levels of trust. They outperform by 286%.[9] Employees have a higher level of satisfaction and are more creative and innovative. Relationships are better as there is more effective, honest communication and information sharing, and leaders can gain more desirable responses from employees. Other benefits of trusting relationships include improved organizational communication, understanding and commitment, increased productivity, and improved self-esteem of both the leader and the employee.[10]

One healthcare facility realized these measurable results of trust.[11] In an effort to improve its culture, the organization addressed trust by hosting a meeting with future leaders. They determined trust was affecting speed and costs. An increase in trust improved speed while lowering costs; a decrease in trust yielded the opposite results—lower speed and higher costs. Participants assessed they could measure trust relative to increase in patient or customer satisfaction, repeat customers, and referrals. As they brainstormed and implemented ideas for improving the community's trust, they realized the following results: lower costs of services, improved customer satisfaction, smoother operations, and renewed confidence that the patients received the right information about their needed care.

Where Trust Begins

When employees follow their leaders, they are trusting them to make decisions for the betterment of themselves, their organization, and community-at-large.[12] Therefore, leaders have to build a culture based on trust, fairness, and integrity, which requires leaders to be responsible, authentic, ethical and honest.[13] In this trusting, leader-follower relationship, trust begins with the writing of the job description and the first phone call between a recruiter and employee candidate. The trust evaluation continues throughout the interviewing and onboarding processes and life cycle of the relationship.

The employee is making a major decision regarding his career and livelihood, affecting not only his work life but also his family and community. Therefore, the organization's hiring team (e.g., recruiter, HR personnel, interviewers, and direct leadership chain) needs to ensure an accurate representation of the organization and job description. For example, job descriptions can have a textbook-like description of the role, as if the position could be cookie-cutter to fit in other organizations regardless of industry; however, the reality may be that neither the company nor the team are set up to enable the fulfillment of the role. Also, during the exploring process, if the candidate has questions that no one can answer, the interviewers should say so and follow up later versus making up responses.

Clyde had earned the title of senior engineer in his current job, and a recruiter invited him to apply for an engineer position at a new company. While he was aware of the difference in job title on paper, out of curiosity, he applied and was selected for the interview. During the interview, he asked about the title and hierarchy; the hiring manager stated that senior engineer titles did not exist in the organization. Understanding there were differences as the firm was in a different industry, Clyde accepted the answer and eventually the position. During his first day on the job, he discovered there were senior engineer roles in the company. While smiling and keeping his composure, there was internal turmoil as Clyde debated within himself about staying, confronting the issue, or answering the calls of the other recruiters who continued to court him. He elected to remain, saying nothing. He worked hard, and his boss eventually promoted him to senior engineer. However, he never received the promised compensation adjustments; therefore, Clyde finally resigned. Would things have been different for Clyde if he had addressed the title issue at the beginning of his tenure? Was the interview exchange about title an indicator of mistrust? To what extent did the level of mistrust uncovered on the first day affect his performance and ultimate success at the company as Clyde spent some of his energy self-protecting and dealing with the emotional challenges associated with this mistrust?

Leaders and HR professionals owe trust to employees and prospects, communicating and living truth at all times (e.g., giving accurate information and keeping promises). In like manner, leaders are looking to trust employees. Credentials marketed on resumes and during interviews must be accurate with candidates and staff members having the knowledge, skills, and experiences as expected and representative of their degrees and certifications. Leaders need to know they can trust their employees to have the competence and commitment to deliver quality work at the agreed-upon time.[14] They need reliability—trust and competence—from their employees, while leading by example.

Leadership Qualities for Building Trust

Over the past forty years or more, Americans have been quickly losing their trust among themselves, businesses, religious institutions, and government.[15] A 2017 Davis Associates report showed that only 43% of employees trusted their leaders.[16] Trust has been a significant missing ingredient amid all the corporate greed, selfishness, abuse and misuse of power, and corporate scandals (e.g., Enron, WorldCom).[17] This void of trust requires leaders, no matter their personal history or "trust" performance, to work together to rebuild trust in the workplace.[18]

There are several qualities leaders need to possess before their employees trust them. First, they are to be compassionate and caring, and show their trustworthiness through authenticity, morality, ethics, fairness, and competence.[19] Leaders also gain employees' trust with vision, influence toward shared goals, and respectful conduct and actions. Employees need to see that their leaders are not all talk but are committed to the organization and its goals and policies. They need leaders who are honest and walk with integrity.[20] When employees experience this trusted leadership, they can become stakeholders, having an ownership mindset with a commitment to the betterment of the organization, which also can enable a leader's trust in their employees.

How to Build and Maintain Trust

Building trust is a continuous, never-ending process that begins with the leader.[21] Building trust requires the leader to align his words and actions.[22] Through consistent behavior of perceived fairness, trust is born.[23] Key elements in building trust include the following (in no order of priority):

1. Being trustworthy in character and principles. Leaders keep promises made and communicate quickly when there are challenges to meeting commitments.[24] Leaders need to adhere genuinely to standards of ethics and integrity.[25]
2. Leading by example. Competent leaders know their role.[26] In their walking the walk and talking the talk, they demonstrate what they want to see in their staff.[27] This effort enables them to earn trust, support, and credibility among employees and other stakeholders.
3. Maintaining open, two-way communication. Leaders are ineffective when they do not listen to others or do not allow others to communicate with them (i.e., one-way communication).[28] Effective leaders encourage two-way dialogue and interaction. To maintain trust, leaders listen and observe both the external indicators and their own inner person warning them of the possibility of losing trust, and then address the issues.[29]
4. Maintaining honest communication. There is truthful dialogue between leaders and followers with no deceit or falsehood.[30]
5. Engaging in personal interaction and involvement. Leaders take the time to get to know their employees and build rapport without getting too involved.[31] Leaders respect and value their employees as human beings who are not perfect, showing interest, care, and concern for their welfare.
6. Acknowledging wrong. Leaders acknowledge when they have made a mistake and make amends to mitigate the risk of losing trust.[32] They take full responsibility for their actions and go the extra mile to ensure trust. There is more than a surface apology, but a genuine desire and effort to take the necessary time for healing and restoration in the relationship.

7. Sharing information and knowledge. Leaders promote trust when they share information, knowledge, and experiences to help guide their team.[33] As trust is built, confidence, truth, and mutual respect prevail.[34] Leaders and employees are free to share information and ideas without fear of criticism, prejudices, or hidden agendas. When sharing information, leaders and followers also maintain confidentiality as needed or requested.
8. Making wise decisions. Organizations expect leaders to manage resources efficiently in reaching corporate goals; therefore, leaders need to be strategic in making wise decisions for corporate sustainability, which also affects employees' wellbeing. Employees find it easier to follow leaders when they make sound business sense.
9. Administering fair treatment and organizational justice. Employees need to know they are being treated fairly.[35] This fairness facilitates their having a positive attitude regarding their boss, their job, and their projects. This positive attitude will be reflected during interactions with their manager.
10. Promoting trust within the team. Leaders influence others as they lead; they model "trust" by example. Leaders do not allow or participate in any form of gossip, and they also manage conflict among the staff.

Conclusion

Trust takes time and can yield incredible benefits. Without it, relationships are strained, unproductive, and do not enable the extraordinary success that can be achieved individually and collectively. Leaders have the primary responsibility to initiate and create a trusting workplace, being the example.[36] However, no matter how hard a leader or employee works towards a trusted leader-follower relationship, one has to acknowledge that sometimes previous experiences or relationships can affect or influence trust on both sides—the leader and follower.[37] For example, if an employee had an abusive or toxic boss in the past, he may expect similar behavior from a future boss; and therefore, become guarded, hindering his contributions to the team, and creating a strained relationship with the new boss—the exact opposite of what they want. Nevertheless, each person has to do his part and be the trusted player in the relationship, contributing to a win-win-win culture.

Chapter 2 - The Trust ACT

Assess Your Attitude & Actions

Based on the content of this chapter, assess your leadership and influence in promoting a trusting work environment.

Chapter 2 Assessment	1	2	3	4	5
Rating Scale: 1=Strongly Disagree 2=Disagree 3=Neutral 4=Agree 5=Strongly Agree					
My organization promotes trust, beginning with the senior leadership and requiring mutual trust at every level.					
I am trustworthy as reflected in my words and actions.					
I promote trust among my staff, peers, superiors, and stakeholders, encouraging mutual trust in words and actions.					

Commit to Personal & Organizational Changes

Based on what you know and have read regarding trust and your personal assessment above, what are you committing to improve for yourself, your staff, peers, superiors, stakeholders, or others?

Commitment	Commitment Date	Target Date
1.		
2.		
3.		

Transform Your Thoughts

*"Trust is the highest form of human motivation.
It brings out the very best in people."*
Stephen R. Covey, Author[38]

*"Few things help an individual more than to place responsibility upon him,
and to let him know that you trust him."*
Booker T. Washington, Educator[39]

"Earn trust, earn trust, earn trust. Then you can worry about the rest."
Seth Godin, Author and Businessman[40]

Leaders ACT to THRIVE!

CHAPTER 3

Health for a Thriving Culture

"Developing a good, healthy culture is extremely important… it directly affects the success of a company's hiring practices and overall strategy."
SCOTT WEISS, BUSINESSMAN & AUTHOR[1]

TONY, A SOFTWARE engineer, was the new kid on the block as he started his second position within the same company. His team was geographically dispersed, split between two states, New York and Delaware. His first boss, Joan, was located in Delaware with him; however, once the boss transitioned to a new position, Tony began to report to a boss in New York. As the newcomer, he was also the youngest with at least a ten-year age difference between him and his peers.

While his teammates were always very helpful, mentoring and coaching him when necessary, they were also protective in a healthy way. For example, on a business trip, a colleague made a sarcastic remark to Tony. One of his peers, Sally, told the boss, Reggie. A few days later, after returning to the office from the trip, Tony received a call from Reggie, asking if he was all right. Surprised by the question, Tony inquired about the reason for the question and learned the details. While he was okay, he appreciated the level of sensitivity and care his team and boss displayed, promoting a healthy culture.

About two years after joining the team, Tony got married. He had not accrued enough vacation time and asked Reggie to work with him on his schedule (i.e., allow him to make up his hours after the honeymoon). Because of the favor his boss showered on him, Tony completed a significant project over a weekend. He moved an application and database to another server to enable a more efficient application that supported equipment engineers. All diagnostics and testing showed that he completed everything successfully. Tony's boss commended him for taking on such a monumental project to make up his time versus just completing minor tactical job requirements.

When Monday rolled around, Tony received a call from Larry, his engineer POC (point of contact) and internal customer in Maryland, asking him questions about the application. Everything seemed to operate fine; however, all data and equipment orders were not there. Tony researched and researched and could not determine a problem. A day passed by with no answers. Finally, on Tuesday, Tony had no choice but to communicate to his boss he had made a mistake and he could not determine the problem nor the solution. He had tried everything he knew and could not get it resolved. The boss handled the news extremely well and immediately asked one of the senior software engineers, Ellen, to work with Tony. Ellen and Tony discussed everything that he had done over the weekend in moving the application and database, and everything he did on Monday to research the problem. Ellen looked and looked, but she too could not determine the root cause of the problem or a solution. In the meantime, Tony was communicating with Larry on status. Larry was exceptionally patient, working with his engineers to keep them calm and productive without escalating to higher management. However, he had to inform Tony of his plans to escalate to his boss if there was not a resolution by the end of the day on Wednesday. Tony was thankful for Larry's patience and understood his position.

As Ellen could not determine a solution, she asked another senior-level peer, Sandra, to review the problem. During Sandra's analysis, she quickly assessed the problem, which stemmed from not compressing the database before transferring it to the other server. Tony was able to redo the database transfer before the deadline, and everyone was happy.

Tony appreciated the teamwork of his peers, and the support and patience from Larry and his boss, Reggie. Tony apologized to everyone for his error. His boss told him that the main thing was that he learned something. Even though the problem had affected the entire group of engineers for three days, no one discussed it again. No one criticized Tony or made him feel bad about the situation. He was even surprised that Reggie did not include or discussed the situation during his performance evaluation. What rang in his ear constantly was his boss' comment, "The main thing is that you learned something."

While this boss and team were not perfect, they operated in a healthy culture of efficiently working together as a team, managing a balanced life. Everyone looked out for each other even though they were a geographically dispersed team. For this reason, they reached their team goals; they grew professionally both individually and collectively, and they supported each other during the happy occasions (e.g., weddings, birthdays) and the sad times (e.g., funerals). They cared, and they all knew it. Tony thrived in his role because he was working in a healthy, win-win-win (although not perfect) culture.

So, what does healthy mean? *The American Heritage Dictionary of the English Language* defines health as "the overall condition of an organism at a given time... soundness, especially of body or mind; freedom from disease or abnormality... a condition of optimal well-being."[2] And, when expanding the topic to explore healthcare, it is "the prevention, treatment, and management of illness and the preservation of mental and physical well-being through the services offered by the medical and allied health professions."[3]

Applying these definitions to the organization, the workplace culture has to be a healthy environment that promotes physical, mental, emotional, and intellectual health for the good of the organization and its primary asset, the people. To this end, leaders own healthcare, being the physicians and healthcare professionals to prevent a dysfunctional, unhealthy culture, and where there is "illness," determine and treat the root cause. Unfortunately, some leaders are the sources of dysfunctionality and toxicity. Therefore, senior leaders and board members have to hold each other and all personnel (i.e., leaders, managers, and employees at every level) accountable to healthy behavior, removing cancer before it spreads, and developing the diet and regimen for a thriving, healthy culture. Leaders can create and promote this healthy culture as they feed the work environment with these nutritional ingredients:

- Personal Health and Work-Life Harmony
- Effective Communication
- Growth in Learning
- Technology Health
- Healthy Conflict Management
- No Fear Here Operation
- Courageous Leadership and Followership

Personal Health and Work-Life Harmony

Healthcare benefits used to be one of the key reasons people sought employment. With rising healthcare costs, organizations struggle and strategize on what is the best solution for the employees while managing costs for the organization. For some companies, healthcare coverage is evolving to being a value-added, competitive differentiation and may even include discounts for healthy lifestyles, going the extra mile to offer discounts on gym memberships and other healthy activities. All significant benefits.

Promoting personal health has to go even further with leaders and organizations enabling work-life harmony. When there are limited resources, leaders do not always strategically assess projects to determine the best use of resources (e.g., financial and human). They may say yes to everything their upper management requests without realizing or addressing the costs. For example, employees spend a lot of time trying to keep up at the expense of sleep, exercise, diet, missed or canceled doctors' appointments, and other obligations to family and community. At some point, the body says, "If you don't rest me or take care of me, I will do it myself." So, the body shuts down through cold, flu, ulcers, heart disease, and other health issues and disorders. At which time, their illness affects the timely realization of the goals assigned, and dependent on the illness, contribute to the rising healthcare costs. Basically, no one wins.

In an ideal work environment with a healthy culture, the leaders and managers at all levels understand the man-hours they have to manage strategically and assign projects accordingly. This strategic allocation of resources does not eliminate the need for flexibility and teamwork— working extra time for critical initiatives like product launches, customer issues, ad hoc projects, and other emergencies. However, these activities are the exceptions and not the norm, and sometimes, the team can expect and plan for them by nature of the event (e.g., software releases). Nevertheless, while enabling health through work-life harmony may not prevent all illnesses or other disruptions, if leaders and employees work together as a team, they can help to minimize the effects of these health challenges, being part of the solution and not contributors to the problem.

Effective Communication

Years ago, when children got upset about something someone said to them, adults would sometimes quote the adage, "Sticks and stones may break my bones, but words will never hurt me." People do not cite this phrase as much today because words hurt. Words have power. Words can build people up or tear them down. Sometimes victims require years or a lifetime to heal from the wounds of words.

Leaders today are to not only promote effective and constructive communication in the workplace, they have to lead by example, ensuring their conversation can influence people toward a positive end. Conversely, ineffective, destructive, and poorly timed communication can negatively affect the mental and emotional health of employees, contributing to an unhealthy culture.

Two of the most challenging times for communication include crisis management and feedback delivery. Leaders have to be careful in the words they use, the tone of delivery, and their nonverbal communication. Leaders have to know their audience— their demographics and national cultures—to ensure they deliver the message in the context and spirit they intended. Leaders must manage emotions regardless of the feelings others display. For example, sarcasm, loud volume, and foul language should not characterize the leaders' communication style. As people have diverse views of foul language and its benefits in the workplace,[4] why not err on the side of being positive? Leaders should strive to leave a favorable "emotional wake, aftermath, aftertaste, or afterglow"—what people remember and feel when the other person is not present.[5]

When sharing feedback in a healthy organization, employees should always know where they stand with their superiors. Information shared during evaluations or coaching sessions must not be surprising to them. They should know if they are doing a great job and where they need to improve performance. Sometimes, there may not be a performance issue but a misunderstanding of preferences; therefore, the leader has to communicate effectively to minimize these challenges. Whether communicating good feedback or growth areas, the leader has to deliver the message in a way that leaves the individual whole and encouraged.

Growth in Learning

Ted was an inspiring executive at a Fortune 100 company and well-respected throughout the organization as he led a staff comprising thousands of employees. The mentioning of his name, his spoken word in a meeting, or a voice message from him commanded one's attention. One day he encouraged his team by saying, "I can't promise to keep you employed, but I can ensure you will always be employable." He was committed to equipping employees with the tools to meet the challenges of their current jobs and future career goals, providing them with the training and growth assignments to keep them marketable internally and externally. Everyone wins in a learning environment. Please refer to the chapters on holism and innovation for more information about this topic.

Technology Health

Technology has had a significant impact on people's lives personally and professionally, improving productivity, and enabling globalization, real-time communication, business continuity, and so much more. However, technology has had negative benefits as well. Before the days of laptops and smartphones, the meeting chair could host a meeting, having the undivided attention of all colleagues as they came prepared and participated in the meeting. When attending meetings today, there are open laptops and phones on the table as managers and leaders multitask, affecting the quality of their contributions, and overall meeting effectiveness; and, therefore, costly to the organization.

Employees have become heavily reliant on emails and instant messaging such that people hardly pick up the phone for a necessary conversation. For example,

Helen was a remote, part-time project manager. When communicating with the team, she would ask questions through emails. It could take three to four days to resolve an issue when a resolution could have been accomplished in one five-minute phone conversation.

When managing geographically dispersed teams, leaders have to assess when to show up. Teleconferencing is excellent for convenience and cost-effectiveness, but employees still enjoy seeing and interacting with their leaders in person when possible. Leaders and employees also have to use other communication technologies effectively. Does an email require an immediate response that could hinder personal productivity? Does instant messaging hinder proper planning? Are people hiding behind technology when communicating, making statements with words, tone and attitude they would not use if speaking on the phone or in-person?

Leaders and employees have to decide who is in charge. Are they leading technology or is technology leading them? Who is controlling what, or what is controlling who? There has to be a right balance of using technology for improved productivity, effectiveness, and communication versus too much reliance on technology that hinders communication, productivity, and effectiveness.

Healthy Conflict Management

Another familiar quote says, "If two people agree on everything, one of them is unnecessary."[6] Leaders and employees are to expect conflict in a healthy relationship and work environment as conflict can facilitate creative problem solving, leading to innovative products and services.[7] In conflict management, they need to distinguish between the person and the problem. There can be conflict relative to the task or problem with various ideas for resolution versus conflict relative to personality or relationship, creating friction and frustration and therefore, a distraction to success.

Healthy organizations focus on the subject or task to yield the best ideas towards an innovative solution—a positive outcome of conflict management. Relationship conflict can have a negative impact on the team or organization, hindering effective and creative exchange of information, knowledge, and decision-making, distracting the focus from the primary goal; therefore, leaders have to resolve the issues quickly. The resolution is also necessary to build and maintain trust within the team as the lack of trust can hinder the sharing of information.

No Fear Here Operation

If a person drives over the speed limit or does not obey traffic signs, jeopardizing people's lives, he should be afraid when he sees the flashing lights behind him or receive a traffic citation in the mail showing he was caught on camera and must pay the fees. Guilty as charged. However, if the same person obeys the traffic laws, has a valid driver's license, and the automobile meets all the proper registrations and safety compliances, he has no fear, and can enjoy a leisure drive on a Sunday afternoon with no worries. Even if stopped, the conscience is clear. Likewise, in the workplace, employees who are abiding by the rules and regulations of the organization and performing their jobs well should have no fear. Yes, there may be times of concern (or fear) regarding pending layoffs, organizational changes, or other unknowns; however, no employee should fear any form of mistreatment, abuse, workplace bullying, unfairness, or unhealthy interaction with his boss or other personnel. They can experience a peaceful environment when their leaders and HR department are policing or nurturing their workplace to ensure no unhealthy fear exists, leading by example and not inflicting any fear.

Dori Meinert, in a *HRMagazine* article entitled "Scared Stiff," shares that fear is infiltrating the workplace, especially during economic downturns when leaders expect employees to do more with less.[8] Some leaders are taking on a "command-and-control" leadership style, creating measurements and processes for achieving the aggressive, unrealistic goals, and setting repercussions if not met. This fear is a hindrance to productivity, and people do not work effectively together. Employees are also more stressed, less engaged, and absent more often. Distrust also prevails.

Signs of fear in the organization include silence during meetings and employees only doing what leaders expect—nothing more. They do not share or challenge ideas, and they may leave the organization. Leaders and HR professionals can combat this fear by building trust, respecting and appreciating employees, improving communication, promoting and rewarding risk-taking and courageous actions. Leaders have to prevent or stop the bleeding of fear before it saturates the entire organization. Treating people well will yield a safe, happier environment where people are loyal, motivated, and productive in achieving goals, and feel good about their accomplishments.

Courageous Leadership and Followership

While a healthy culture is void of fear, a healthy culture promotes a spirit of courage. Fear is crippling; it hinders and stunts growth while courage promotes growth and creates a win-win-win. As employees have a natural propensity to respect and submit to authority within the workplace, and organizations have a protocol for how employees interact with their leaders, whether formally or informally, leaders need to promote a courageous leader-follower relationship.[9]

Organizations can create a culture where followers are free to be authentic in their interactions with their leaders. Followers also are to be comfortable enough to take the initiative, take risks, give feedback, or influence decisions. They are committed to the overall success of the organization, which empowers their courageous actions. For example, Brian and his marketing communications teammates worked in a healthy work environment and did not fear leadership. Their boss tasked them to develop a presentation for Ron, the senior vice president of sales, to deliver to the entire employee body. Ron also provided a slide to include. The team immediately assessed that the slide was incorrect and someone needed to address the issue with Ron. When they met with Ron to walk through the draft presentation, Brian had the courage to share feedback regarding the slide. Ron appreciated the information but said he still wanted the slide in the presentation. However, when Ron delivered the message, he introduced and discussed the slide in a way that averted any negativity. Brian was pleased with the executive's delivery and thankful that he had spoken up. It is a mystery regarding what would have happened if Brian had not shared the concern about the slide. Would there have been an embarrassing moment for the executive? Would Ron have questioned the team for not saying anything? Would this exchange and lack of honesty be the beginning of distrust in the leader-follower relationship? When leaders and followers are courageous, they can unite in yielding results for the betterment of the organization.

Conclusion

Leaders are the physicians, health officials, and police officers in the organization responsible for maintaining a healthy, safe environment for all personnel at all levels so that the entire organization can live and thrive. They ensure fear, ineffective communication, or any form of abusive behavior are not tolerated in the organization to any degree. They also promote courage, learning, and personal growth among the employees. Because of leaders taking care of employees in a healthy culture, employees take care of their leaders in achieving results. In essence, when leaders focus on the health of the organization, they facilitate a healthy environment to yield a healthy performance—products, services, employee and customer satisfaction, and ROI for the betterment of employees, customers, shareholders, and the community-at-large for the win-win-win. Everyone thrives!

Chapter 3 - The Health ACT

Assess Your Attitude & Actions

Based on the content of this chapter, please assess your leadership and influence in promoting a healthy work environment.

Chapter 3 Assessment	1	2	3	4	5
Rating Scale: 1=Strongly Disagree 2=Disagree 3=Neutral 4=Agree 5=Strongly Agree					
My organizational culture is healthy at all levels.					
I enjoy work-life harmony, and I enable a healthy work environment, ensuring my attitude, words and actions have a positive influence on others.					
I promote a healthy corporate culture and business practices in the workplace among my staff, peers, superiors, stakeholders, and customers. I hold them accountable in ensuring their attitude, words and actions have a positive influence on others.					

Commit to Personal & Organizational Changes

Based on what you know and have read regarding corporate health and your personal assessment above, what are you committing to improve for yourself, your staff, peers, superiors, stakeholders, or others?

Commitment	Commitment Date	Target Date
1.		
2.		
3.		

Transform Your Thoughts

"A hallmark of a healthy creative culture is that its people feel free to share ideas, opinions, and criticisms. Lack of candor, if unchecked, ultimately leads to dysfunctional environments."
Ed Catmull, Former President, Pixar[10]

"To win in the marketplace, you must first win in the workplace."
Doug Conant, Former President & CEO, Campbell Soup[11]

"Everybody blames the culture without taking responsibility."
James Levine, Musician[12]

"If we are to preserve culture, we must continue to create it."
Johan Huizinga, Historian[13]

Leaders Act to THRIVE!

CHAPTER **4**

Respect from the Heart to Thrive

*"Every human being, of whatever origin, of whatever station, deserves respect.
We must each respect others even as we respect ourselves."*
RALPH WALDO EMERSON, ESSAYIST, LECTURER, AND POET[1]

THE LATE M. Scott Peck, the author of *The Different Drum*, shared in the prologue of his book a believed-to-be myth entitled "The Rabbi's Gift."[2] This story is about a monastery, which was experiencing some difficulties due to anti-monastic persecutions and other devastations, leaving only one abbot and four monks who were all over seventy years of age. The monastery also had a visiting neighbor, the rabbi, who had a hut in the deep woods where he occasionally used as a hermitage. The monks knew when he visited and would whisper among themselves "the rabbi is in the woods."[3]

One day the abbot decided to visit the rabbi. The rabbi welcomed him with open arms, and they had a great conversation. Before the abbot left, he asked the rabbi for wisdom regarding how to revive and save the monastery. The rabbi had no advice to share but stated, "The only thing I can tell you is the Messiah is one of you."[4] The abbot relayed this statement to his fellow monks.

As the monks pondered the message, they contemplated if this comment was true and if it was, who might be the Messiah. They examined each person and could see how any of the four could be the one, enabling them to recognize and appreciate their virtues. When they thought of themselves as the possible Messiah, they humbly felt they were not good enough. In questioning the "who," they treated each other and themselves with exceptional respect. This new atmosphere of respect was so inviting that the occasional visitors who came by to enjoy the beauty of the forest, have picnics, pray, play and walk along the trails, invited others who also encouraged their friends and family members to come. The extraordinary respect was contagious! Young men also started coming and asking to join the monastery. Within a few years, the monastery was thriving again, all because of the gift of respect they gave themselves and each other.

Respect is an essential element in any relationship while disrespect can be costly. As people spend most of their productive time in the workplace, respect or the lack thereof can have a significant impact on one's personal and professional wellbeing. Paul Meshanko, the author of *The Respect Effect*, argues there are five reasons respect is essential in the workplace:[5]

1. Social Justice: It is the right thing to do regardless of who the people are.
2. Biology: Respect triggers the right neurons, electrical impulses, and neurotransmitters to cause the brain to perform at its best. Disrespect causes the brain to fall asleep.
3. Employee Engagement: There is an improvement in employee involvement with emotional commitment to succeed for the organization, which is also a personal victory.
4. Costs: In 2018, according to the U.S. Equal Employment Opportunity Commission (EEOC), settlements totaled over $505 million due to discrimination,[6] not including associated legal and attorney fees, and out-of-court settlements.[7] Other costs to corporations included low productivity and morale, and negative impact on goodwill.
5. Personal Legacy: Fast forward five to ten years or more into the future. People may not remember discussions during staff meetings, all the team victories, or one's hard work. They will remember how one made them feel—happy, confident, intimidated, supported, inferior, motivated—the impressions that can last a lifetime.

Respect is defined as "an active process of nonjudgmentally engaging people from all backgrounds. It is practiced to increase [one's] awareness and effectiveness and demonstrated in a manner that esteems [oneself] and those with whom [one] interact[s]."[8] It is the appreciation or deferential regard one has for another.[9] Respect should be extended to everyone; and therefore, there must be a distinction from esteem, liking, or admiration.[10] Another way to understand respect is to think about what it eliminates—the treatment of people for selfish gain, using people only as a means to an end, and forgetting their humanity or personhood. "Respect is an important component of both personal self-identity and interpersonal relationships. Feeling respected can almost be considered a basic human right."[11]

Respecting others includes valuing them for who they are, allowing them to be themselves with their own needs, wants, desires, and purposes, and appreciating their decisions and values.[12] Respect is treating people with "an unconditional worth and valuable individual differences," and providing an opportunity for followers to integrate their needs, values, and purposes with those of the leader. It requires listening, empathy, and welcoming of conflicting views. Respect is the special sauce for enabling a thriving workplace with a win-win-win culture—an atmosphere of belonging, acceptance, and enjoyment. People respect and embrace the individuality of each member of the diverse culture. They recognize and respect their differences in a safe, welcoming environment.

This all sounds wonderful, right? How does an organization get there? Key elements leaders can promote within the organization to enable a rich culture of respect are:

- Genuine Respect Deserved By All
- Personal Awareness and Ongoing Personal Introspection
- Acknowledgement and Respect for Diversity
- Adherence to the Golden Rule - Expanded Edition
- No Tolerance for Disrespect
- Adherence to a Code of Mutual Respect
- Training and Understanding of Cultural Differences

Genuine Respect Deserved By All

No matter who the person is—their nationality, ethnicity, gender, faith, or economic status—all leaders and employees have to understand and appreciate that every human being deserves respect and should expect respect. Regardless of their educational achievements, rank or position in the organization, or affiliation with any renowned person, all persons from janitorial staff to mailroom personnel to the CEO are due respect. Howard Schultz, former Chairman and CEO of Starbucks, shares, "[We treat] employees with respect and dignity, both because we have a team of leaders who believe it's right and because it's the best way to do business... We treat warehouse workers and entry-level retail people with the kind of respect most companies show for only high executives."[13]

This respect cannot be a check-the-box kind of respect, just general niceties, or the out-of-duty requirement. It needs to be genuine and come from the heart. People need to feel they matter and are not just being tolerated. They need to know they are important not for what they do but for who they are—human beings, God's valuable, precious creations. This respect is shown in one-on-one interactions, a look in the eye, firm handshake, smile, thank you, acceptance, fairness, and decisions. Everything said and done must be bathed with respect and seasoned with genuine love for one another.

Personal Awareness and Ongoing Personal Introspection

Respect in the workplace begins with the leaders. To respect and build a culture of respect, leaders have to be real with themselves. Am I respectful? Do others respect me? When am I not respecting others? Is there a pattern to my disrespect of others? Is it relative to my stress level, emotional state, or geared towards certain individuals? To whom am I disrespectful, and why? Am I prejudice? Do stereotypes influence how I treat people? Are there personal insecurities or personal pride affecting my treatment of others? Am I pleased with my attitude and actions in respecting others? Do I want or need to change my behavior in any way?

Answering these sensitive questions is challenging, but they help get to the core as leaders set the tone for how followers or even other leaders behave; therefore, respect has to be the priority for the day—every day. As no one is perfect, when outward displays of disrespect occur, the person has to acknowledge the behavior and apologize. If there is an inner struggle (not displayed publicly), he can deal with it privately, seeking counsel if needed; there is no need to apologize to others. In both cases, change is necessary; there is no reason to remain the same. Everyone will be better for it.

Acknowledgement and Respect for Diversity

Everyone is different. Two people from the same family with the same biological parents are not exactly alike. On the surface, there are noticeable similarities, but deep down inside, there are striking differences because over the years, their lives have been affected separately by experiences, academics, relationships, challenges, and the list goes on—all contributing to each one's uniqueness. For leaders and organizations to succeed, they have to figure out how to leverage this diversity for the good of the people, including the customers they serve, and the company as a whole. Leaders have to acknowledge and respect diversity and help everyone else to do the same.

When addressing diversity, sometimes people find the discussion of race difficult.[14] In their effort to pseudo deal with it, they adopt a mindset of "color blindness," which is "the racial ideology that posits the best way to end discrimination is by treating individuals as equally as possible, without regard to race, culture, or ethnicity."[15] On the surface, this mindset sounds good as it appears to promote Dr. Martin Luther King, Jr.'s vision of not judging people by their skin color but by who they are— "the content of their character." They try to find common ground by looking at the similarities everyone shares as human beings.

The challenge with this color-blind mindset is that it can perpetuate racism as members of the majority will not feel discrimination and therefore dismiss racism while minorities continue to experience the effects. "Color blindness creates a society that denies their negative racial experiences, rejects their cultural heritage, and invalidates their unique perspectives." When racial challenges occur, color blindness prevents people from seeing the big picture (e.g., values, stereotypes, cultural differences) affecting the problem. Without full knowledge or awareness, the right solution cannot be determined.

Paul Meshanko, author of book, *The Respect Effect: Using the Science of Neuroleadership to Inspire a More Loyal and Productive Workplace*, experienced this color blindness, believing adherence to the Golden Rule allowed him to wish away prejudges, stereotypes, and social injustice or inequalities, and treat everyone the same.[16] However, Dale Linder, his dorm director, an African American male, six years older than Paul, helped him open his eyes. Dale said, "'Paul, we are not the same. If you won't acknowledge our differences and what those might mean, then you can't really respect me.'"[17] Paul concluded, "By intentionally failing to acknowledge Dale's blackness and other differences, I was treating him with disrespect… Dale helped me see him as a unique individual. By seeing others as they are, black, white, short, tall, Asian, Indian, old or young, docile or angry, we acknowledge them, and all that makes them unique. Only through discovering and acknowledging what they are can we genuinely understand and respect who they are."[18]

Like the lesson Paul learned, Mellody Hopson, in her TED Talk, "Color Blind or Color Brave," invites people to be color brave. She says, at work, home, school, everywhere, people "have to be willing to have proactive conversations about race with honesty and understanding and courage."[19] Dr. Monnica Williams shares similar views, stating it is time to change and see.[20] It is time to embrace "multiculturalism, an ideology that acknowledges, highlights, and celebrates ethnoracial differences. It recognizes that each tradition has something valuable to offer. It is not afraid to see how others have suffered as a result of racial conflict or differences." Steps toward multiculturalism include acknowledging and appreciating the differences, learning the differences, and building relationships. This change is difficult and takes time, but must be done.

Besides people diversity, leaders also have to acknowledge and respect the diversity of skills and positions. While there is a natural inclination to honor and appreciate people who are business leaders and owners, lawyers, and doctors, organizations also have to acknowledge and respect the diverse skills at all levels as they contribute to the success of the organization. The diversity of skills, backgrounds, and experiences adds value to the team; therefore, everyone needs to respect and value their unique contributions no matter how big or small. Also, no one should belittle or exalt one position over the other. Humility along with respect must prevail.

Adherence to the Golden Rule - Expanded Edition

In any relationship, people can use the Golden Rule as a guiding principle in treating others the way they desire to be treated. No matter one's culture, religious background, social status, or ethnicity, everyone understands the Golden Rule.[21] However, to be most effective in relating and respecting others with diverse backgrounds, one has to walk in another's shoes to determine how best to apply the Golden Rule.[22] Taking the Golden Rule Quiz (Exhibit 4.1) can help to assess if one's desired behaviors are effective when relating with others.

Exhibit 4.1

The Golden Rule Quiz	
Read each statement and put an X next to those that describe how you would like to be treated.	
1. I prefer a person with whom I am speaking to look me in the eyes when he or she talks to me.	
2. I would want a friend to accept and open a gift that I give to him or her.	
3. I would not want to be interrupted when I am speaking.	
4. I would want a colleague to actively listen when I am presenting.	
5. I would want to be acknowledged for my professional accomplishments.	
6. I expect my colleagues to respect my time and not be late.	
7. I prefer to be judged at work by my character and knowledge, not by my appearance.	
8. I would want my personal space to be respected.	
9. I would not want to be touched by someone I do not know.	
10. I would want to be honest with a colleague if I thought he or she was wrong about a work-related decision.	

Extracted from Caligiuri (2012), 58.

Answering these questions can demonstrate the diversity of thought depending on their national culture, ethnicity, or upbringing; therefore, one has to have a greater understanding of the cultural differences and study their colleagues to know how to respect the differences and work effectively with each other. No one can assume people of the same gender, nationality, profession or other characteristics will think and act the same. Leaders and employees have to take the time to learn more about each other to enhance their application of the Golden Rule, which can be a rewarding and insightful journey.

No Tolerance for Disrespect

As discussed earlier in this chapter, there are definite benefits of having a culture of respect. However, a few seconds of disrespect can destroy what may have taken years to build.[23] When disrespected, people can feel attacked, humiliated, fearful, angry, insecure, disengaged, hopeless, embarrassed, paralyzed, incompetent, and the list goes on.[24] In addition, organizations can witness the following downsides:[25]

- Decreased employee productivity
- Increased stress-related illnesses
- Increased absenteeism and on-the-job accidents
- Inability to adapt to change in a competitive, dynamic marketplace
- Limited, selective communication due to fear
- Lower employee engagement
- Loss of top talent

To counter these challenges and maintain a culture of respect, leaders and employees need to know how to identify and articulate excellent and bad behavior. To this end, the continuum of behavior table (Table 4.1) can facilitate understanding of respectful and disrespectful actions, and the ability to confront disrespectful activities with confidence:[26]

This information should be included in the corporate conduct or culture training program along with guidance for addressing violations. Leaders also have to ensure employees understand their organization does not support toxic and bullying behavior; therefore, everyone has to be encouraged to partner with the organization to promote a respectful culture, having the confidence and the courage to stand against wrong whenever a violation occurs.

Adherence to a Code of Mutual Respect

A Code of Mutual Respect also can be written or incorporated in other corporate conduct documents to define respect and the associated expectations for how employees treat others.[27] The Code of Mutual Respect should include principles regarding professionalism, confidentiality, language, communication, and feedback, and reviewed by a variety of people from different departments and at various levels before implementing it.[28] These guidelines can become the foundation for training while also informing leaders as they lead by example. However, having a document

Table 4.1

Type of Behavior	Respectful Behavior	Continuum of Behavior Disrespectful Behavior: Incivility	Disrespectful Behavior: Intimidation or Bullying	Bad Behavior
Definition	Interpersonal behavior that supports a positive work environment in which all employees can do quality work and enjoy coming to work	Low-intensity deviant behavior that violates workplace norms for mutual respect	A persistent form of hostility	Unacceptable behavior that requires formal policies and procedures
Examples	• Professionalism • Positive collaborative relationships • Courtesy • Listening • Confidentiality, privacy • Prompt, direct feedback • Language, including nonverbal behavior and gestures, that reflects dignity • Frequent, clear communication	• Rudeness • Public embarrassment • Sarcasm • Impatience with questions • Inappropriate remarks about performance in front of others • Delaying or refusing to answer [texts] based on interpersonal relationship issues • Insinuating accusations rather than being direct	• Abusive language • Threats of retribution or litigation • Persistent insults about performance • Berating colleagues • Demeaning subordinates • Threating to ruin a career if behavior is reported • Lashing out randomly at others	• Threats of violence or actual violence • Physical abuse • Sexual harassment, including vulgar, sexually suggestive, or explicit comments • Discriminatory remarks, including racial, ethnic, or religious slurs • Immediate danger to the safety, health, and welfare of others • Criminal activity
Code Process	Reward and encourage	Mediated conversations	Mediated conversations	Discipline, possible loss of privileges
Resources	Users	Leaders	Leaders	Human resources; legal department; policies, procedures, and bylaws

Extracted and Adapted from Kaplan, Mestel, and Feldman (2010), 497.

alone is not good enough. The culture and the code need to enable employees at all levels to feel free and confident to speak up when people do not practice the desired behaviors of respect with no negative repercussions.[29] When people speak up, they help create and maintain a positive work environment with improved productivity, teamwork, employee retention, and customer experience.

Organizations can assess how they are doing by conducting a Code of Mutual Respect Survey (Exhibit 4.2).[30]

Exhibit 4.2

Code of Mutual Respect Survey
Please respond to ALL of the statements below using a scale of 1 to 5 in which 5 means you strongly agree with the statement and 1 means you strongly disagree with the statement.
1. I understand clearly the code of mutual respect.
2. The code of mutual respect has a positive impact on the work environment.
3. The standard of behavior and accountability is the same for all leaders and employees.
4. Leaders address disrespectful behavior effectively.
5. I speak up when I observe people violating the code of mutual respect.
6. My leaders and colleagues treat me with respect.
7. I treat employees with respect in my daily interactions.

Kaplan, Mestel, and Feldman (2010), 503.

This survey should be conducted before launching the program, after any training, and at least once a year. Qualitative feedback can also provide significant learnings as employees become more aware of their behavior, including understanding the triggers that challenge their ability to respect, and how to ward off any levels of disrespect. Keeping the Code of Mutual Respect top of mind in various forms (e.g., training, surveys, and artifacts) can continually promote and encourage the desired behavior.

Training and Understanding of Cultural Differences

Besides training employees on the Code of Mutual Respect and other topics included in this chapter, the training also has to address the attitude and mindset for respecting, valuing, and appreciating the diversity of human cultures.[31] For example, employees do not have to deny their own culture, and they should not believe their culture is the norm or standard. This training can help employees understand that diversity can provide fresh opportunities to achieve greatness while also creating healthy conflict that leads to better solutions.

Training can help employees eliminate stereotypes and cultural comparisons and value the culture diversity.[32] This training has to educate professionals to consider other cultures when making decisions by discussing how majority groups address the needs and wants of the minority groups.[33] They have to understand the complexities and cultural values that can enable favorable outcomes for all.

Conclusion

Respect in the workplace has to be a mandate; not an option. To develop and cultivate a culture of respect, leaders have to personify respect and good leadership as provided in the guidelines for establishing and maintaining a respectful culture (Exhibit 4.3).

Exhibit 4.3

Leadership Guidelines for Establishing & Maintaining a Respectful Culture
1. Show good leadership by being ethical, setting the standards, acting with integrity 24/7, and valuing people.
2. Be accountable by holding oneself and others responsible for behavior and actions.
3. Show respect to all; it is essential.
4. Communicate the expectations of a respectful workplace constantly.
5. Have the courage to do something! Don't just do things right, do the right thing!

Extracted from Maeso (2017), 29.

Leaders have to take the time to know their people, which helps to build trust and open lines of communication.[34] This effective leader-follower relationship equips the leader to be observant and able to sense when something is wrong even though he may not know what is wrong. He can then ask probing questions to get to the root cause or seek help when needed. In essence, leaders set the tone of respect. They, along with employees and fellow leaders, must hold everyone accountable for creating and maintaining a safe, respectful environment wherein everyone respects each other, does not tolerate disrespect at any level but confronts disrespect without retaliation.[35] Leaders must respect from the heart to promote a culture where followers also genuinely respect others.

Chapter 4 - The Respect ACT

Assess Your Attitude & Actions

Based on the content of this chapter, please assess your leadership and influence in promoting a respectful work environment.

Chapter 4 Assessment	1	2	3	4	5
Rating Scale: 1=Strongly Disagree 2=Disagree 3=Neutral 4=Agree 5=Strongly Agree					
My organization promotes a culture of respect, ensuring everyone understands the definition and application of respect, and treats all employees at all levels with respect.					
I respect myself and treat all persons in the organization with respect regardless of who they are—their unique characteristics, talents, skills, titles, positions, or social status. I respect them as human beings and contributing members of the organization. I address any degree of disrespect regardless of the involved persons' positions or my relationship with them.					
I promote respect in the workplace among my staff, peers, superiors, stakeholders, and customers, encouraging them to value and respect every team member, and address any degree of disrespect regardless of the involved persons' positions or their relationship with them.					

Commit to Personal & Organizational Changes

Based on what you know and have read regarding respect and your personal assessment above, what are you committing to improve for yourself, your staff, peers, superiors, stakeholders, or others?

Commitment	Commitment Date	Target Date
1.		
2.		
3.		

THRIVE²

Transform Your Thoughts

*"Respect commands itself and can neither
be given nor withheld when it is due."*
Eldridge Cleaver, Writer and Political Activist[36]

*"I speak to everyone in the same way,
whether he is the garbage man or the president of the university."*
Albert Einstein, Physicist[37]

*"I'm not concerned with your liking or disliking me …
All I ask is that you respect me as a human being."*
Jackie Robinson, Athlete[38]

"Most good relationships are built on mutual trust and respect."
Mona Sutphen, a former White House Deputy Chief of Staff for Policy[39]

*"Respect for ourselves guides our morals,
respect for others guides our manners."*
Laurence Sterne, Novelist & Anglican Clergyman[40]

Leaders ACT to THRIVE!

CHAPTER 5

Image that Thrives

*"There is just no way any management with any intelligence
and foresight cannot recognize the value of a corporate image.
It is the best, single marketable investment that a company can make."*
MALCOLM FORBES, ENTREPRENEUR & PUBLISHER OF FORBES MAGAZINE[1]

CORPORATE IMAGE IS synonymous with corporate reputation.[2] Image represents what people think about or visualize when they hear the company's name. It differs from corporate identity—how the corporation wants people to view them through the company's visual elements (e.g., logo, website, and stationary).[3] Having a good corporate image or reputation can be an asset that can yield higher revenue and stock valuation.[4] Therefore, leaders have to ensure their actions help align image with identity —what people think equals what the company says it is.

Rolex, Lego, the Walt Disney Company, Adidas, and Microsoft are the world's most reputable companies according to the 2019 report by Reputation Institute (RI), a Boston-based reputation management consulting firm,[5] which assesses organizations based on seven categories of corporate reputation.[6] They determined that the corporate views comprising five dimensions (i.e., leadership, governance, workplace, citizenship, and financial performance) are more important than the two product perception factors (i.e., products and services, and innovation). For example, customers purchase, invest, and seek employment based on 60% perceptions of the company and 40% perceptions of the products. Customers relate more with what the companies stand for than what they sell. Companies build strong images by creating and telling their stories to appeal to the people and showing genuine care for the stakeholders. Therefore, companies "need to live up to [their] promises and be relevant in the local and global context."

43

While building a powerful image and reputation takes time, it can be destroyed easily. For example, in 2015, Volkswagen ranked 14th and dropped to 123rd place in 2016 due to the emissions scandal.[7] They improved their rating in 2017, ranking 100;[8] however, they did not make the top 100 list in 2018 and 2019.[9]

An organization can also have several conflicting views from various groups.[10] For example, customers may like a company's brand image while a supplier rates them poorly for being tough negotiators, lacking loyalty, and not paying on time. Investors may love the company but at the cost of closing operations in some cities, yielding a negative image with the community. Employees may also have various perceptions because of their compensation plan while customers enjoy low prices. Essentially, there are many factors that influence the corporate image of which the people and the culture have a major impact.

The leaders and employees create all the elements (e.g., the products, marketing, community service, customer experience) that contribute to the corporate perception that can yield high marks with customers, investors, and the community overall. And, as noted by Jim Collins, author of *Good to Great*, "those who build great companies understand that the ultimate throttle on growth for any company is not markets or technology or competition or products. It is one thing above all others: the ability to get and keep enough of the right people."[11] Therefore, organizations need to employ the right leaders and employees who have the qualities and skills to shape the corporate image and differentiation in the marketplace. Key ingredients to a stellar corporate image include:

- Excellence through Competence
- Customer Experience Enhanced with a Servant Spirit
- Character Excellence and Development
- Positive Attitude

Excellence through Competence

Effective leaders are competent and have proficient people who excel in fulfilling all the functions affecting the corporate image—leadership, governance, workplace, citizenship, financial performance, products and services, and innovation.[12] They have a standard of quality based on best practices as well as going beyond the norm; and, sometimes just the simple exercise of common sense[13] in a spirit of servicing customers and employees. They continue to develop and master their craft such that it aligns with the market.[14] They are committed to excellence wherein all persons at all levels on every aspect of the assignment are giving their best, working as a team and learning from each other.[15] As life and the marketplace change, they also continue to change and grow for personal and corporate sustainability. They are action-oriented, continuing to learn, and using their knowledge to enhance a product, service, or process. Their skills development also includes managing customer relationships, building trust and confidence. Additionally, effective communications skills in writing, presentations development and delivery, and meeting management are critical elements to their success.

Financial stewardship is another major component of excellence along with integrity, quality, and people management.[16] Financially successful organizations have a top-to-bottom commitment. Everyone in the organization operates with integrity, quality, and standards of putting clients first, treating and rewarding employees well, and investing in the right resources.

Customer Experience Enhanced with a Servant Spirit

Jeff Bezos, Amazon CEO, says, "If there's one reason we have done better than our peers…, it is because we have focused like a laser on customer experience."[17] The customer experience, which includes every touch point or engagement with the customer, is a crucial element affecting the corporate image. It influences customer loyalty, customer spending and frequency, word-of-mouth marketing, repeat business, and upsell opportunities.[18] Therefore, organizations must ensure customer service personnel, sales personnel, or anyone engaging with the customer treats them with respect, understands the customers' needs and wants, responds to feedback, resolves problems, and goes beyond the call of duty to help the customer.

Employees must listen attentively to empathize with the customers and understand their needs and wants in the written, verbalized, and unspoken word. They have to translate the information into actionable plans to solve customers' problems and concerns, contributing to a healthy, differentiated corporate image. Also, customers need access to the personnel. Customers should not have to hunt for a telephone number or be forced to research an answer on the corporate website before they can get to the resources who can help them—a challenge no customer should experience if an organization desires to excel in customer service.

Customer experience is also one way organizations can differentiate themselves in the market as noted by Jerry Gregoire, former Dell CIO, who shares, "the customer experience is the next competitive battleground."[19] Therefore, leaders have to look for innovative ways to transform and prepare for the future. Mark Pernice, in a *Harvard Business Review* article states that many times organizations will rewrite the script of the customer-facing employees to improve the corporate experience, resulting in limited change.[20] However, as these employees understand the need to satisfy customers, the better solution is to give them the flexibility and creativity to understand and address the customers' needs, supported by other departments. To this end, all employees, including those in support roles, should receive customer service training with special attention to how they collaboratively serve their internal clients to service the external customers.

This training needs to focus on the definition and application of service excellence—adding value to the customer (internal and external), understanding customers' concerns, and knowing how best to address them. All employees in the organization have to operate with the understanding and mindset that everyone is their customer and have a genuine care for them with a servant's spirit. Everyone focuses—listening attentively and intentionally—to their customers' needs and determine the best way to address them.

Companies with exceptional customer experience have CEOs who make customer-focus a priority.[21] CEOs, along with board members, are intricately involved in facilitating a customer-focused organization wherein people stay abreast of the latest trends in customer experience to remain relevant and competitive. This customer-focused mindset is integrated into every element of the organization—the culture, structure, and process—the main obstacles to the customer experience. Without a doubt, the CEO has a significant role in transforming the company to enable exceptional customer experiences.

As time is a precious commodity, organizations may consider leveraging technology (e.g., artificial intelligence, predictive data, and analytics) to facilitate a personalized customer experience, optimize the opportunity to gather data at every touch point, showcase products and services that fit the customer's specific needs, and foresee red flags. These tools and tactics can facilitate retaining customers, improving satisfaction, and enabling personnel to understand customers' views and needs, and their impact on the corporate image.

Seeking feedback beyond external polls is also helpful. For example, Toyota occasionally conducts surveys to understand customer views of the company. In one study, customers perceived Toyota's presence in the US was decreasing although Toyota had been building and expanding operations in the US.[22] This insight prompted Toyota to put their marketing resources together to communicate their investments in the US. They were doing the work but needed to tell their story—convey their reality to improve customer perceptions.

Character Excellence and Development

As leaders focus on their corporate image, they have to understand that character is just as critical to success as competence.[23] When developing and maintaining a positive corporate image, leaders need to ensure their character, and the character of all personnel, is conducive to the image they want to portray inside and outside of the organization.[24] Leaders not only have to demonstrate good character, they also have to build a culture, which promotes the desired character with consistency in their walk and talk. Essentially, to maintain high performance, one needs "task excellence" and "relational excellence."[25] For example, the late John Wooden, legendary coach of the multiple championship UCLA men's basketball team, trained his players on the principle that one's "'ability may get [him] to the top, but only character will keep [him] there.'" Character matters.

The consistency of character reveals who people are—positive and constructive or negative and destructive.[26] It goes beyond how they manage a crisis or challenging, controversial decisions. Leaders show their character in everything they do—communications, problem-solving, conflict resolution, rewards and disciplines, team selection and team building. There is no difference in their character at work, home, or play. Character remains unwavering regardless of the crisis, political climate, negative opinions, or positive views. The leader's character is consistent as it reflects his heart.

Leaders can help promote and develop the desired character with the five E's of character development as defined by Gene Klann, author of *Building Character: Strengthening the Heart of Good Leadership*:[27]

1. Example: Leaders influence and set the standard for the desired character or behavior of the organization as employees have the tendency to follow and emulate the behavior and actions of people with authority or people they respect and view in high regard.[28]
2. Experience: Leaders and employees also need hands-on experience—opportunities to serve in different capacities or simulated environments.[29] While reading and learning from others can also help, there is nothing like personal experience.[30] They need experiences to facilitate growth in knowledge, skill, and character. Personal and corporate trials also contribute to this growth.[31]
3. Education: Formal and informal training can aid in developing the desired character, dealing with customers, competition, and moral and ethical dilemmas.[32] Employees can identify personal gaps and leverage self-educational opportunities.[33] For some people, self-education is more suitable than formal training programs.
4. Environment: Sometimes leaders have to transform the organizational culture to support the desired character traits of its leaders and employees.[34] The organization's values, beliefs, and priorities will contribute to the environment.[35] Including character development in business plans and strategies with budget also communicates the importance of establishing an environment for the desired character development.[36]

5. Evaluation: People are more attentive to performance criteria as they know leaders will hold them accountable. Having character development activities included in appraisals, coaching sessions, and criteria for merit increases and bonuses will promote a level of accountability while demonstrating the importance of character to the culture and corporate image.[37]

Positive Attitude

Life can get rough sometimes. Employees and customers alike face many challenges at work, home, or community, or worry about national and global issues. Sometimes the problems of the day affect how one person interacts with another, and sometimes one has to decide how to respond to the lemons of life, just as Charles Swindoll, a Christian pastor and author, did when dealing with his personal challenges.[38] He states:

> The longer I live, the more I realize the impact of attitude on life. Attitude, to me is more important than facts. It is more important than the past, than education, than money, than circumstances, than failures, than successes, than what other people think or say or do. It is more important than appearance, giftedness, or skill. It will make or break a company… a church… a home. The remarkable thing is we have a choice every day regarding the attitude we will embrace for that day. We cannot change our past… we cannot change the fact that people will act in a certain way.
>
> We cannot change the inevitable. The only thing we can do is play on the one string we have, and that is our attitude… I am convinced that life is 10% what happens to me and 90% how I react to it. And so it is with you… we are in charge of our attitudes.

A positive attitude enables one to take the high road when under stress or encountering someone with a negative attitude. Specific to the corporate image, the employee is the face of the organization to the customer, and the customer will assess the company based on his or her exchange with the employee despite the employee's level or function.[39] Therefore, a positive attitude will enable a pleasant exchange and powerful image with customers regardless of the situation, even when the customer has made a mistake. Leaders and employees have to take ownership of their attitudes.

Conclusion

A positive corporate image takes time to establish and maintain. Leaders have to ensure they have competent, caring personnel at all levels and especially on the frontline who will genuinely and consistently do the right thing for customers, fellow employees, stakeholders, and the organization. They need to be competent in their business deals and interactions, demonstrating an understanding of the market, financial stewardship, and stellar customer service. They are to have the characteristics of trust, integrity, a strong work ethic, and self-discipline upon which customers, business partners, fellow leaders, and employees can depend. Having these qualities does not mean the organization will be perfect or every customer and employee will always be happy; however, because they are customer-focused with the right intent, they can work toward win-win-win solutions where their public corporate image aligns with their identity. They execute with excellence, exceeding expectations.

Chapter 5 - The Image ACT

Assess Your Attitude & Actions

Based on the content of this chapter, please assess your leadership responsibility and influence in developing and maintaining a positive corporate image.

Chapter 5 Assessment	1	2	3	4	5
Rating Scale: 1=Strongly Disagree 2=Disagree 3=Neutral 4=Agree 5=Strongly Agree					
My organizational culture promotes the character, competence, and excellence needed to affect and maintain a positive corporate image.					
I have the character, competence, and excellence that reflect and influence a positive corporate image.					
I promote and enable a positive corporate image by influencing the desired character, competence and excellence among my staff, peers, superiors, and stakeholders.					

Commit to Personal & Organizational Changes

Based on what you know and have read regarding corporate image and your personal assessment above, what are you committing to improve for yourself, your staff, peers, superiors, stakeholders, or others?

Commitment	Commitment Date	Target Date
1.		
2.		
3.		

Transform Your Thoughts

"It takes 20 years to build a reputation and five minutes to ruin it. If you think about that, you'll do things differently."
Warren Buffett, Businessman[40]

"Character may almost be called the most effective means of persuasion."
Aristotle, Philosopher[41]

"You've got to start with the customer experience and work back toward the technology—not the other way around."
Steve Jobs, Co-Founder of Apple Inc.[42]

Leaders ACT to THRIVE!

CHAPTER 6

Values that Thrive

"The culture of a workplace—an organization's values, norms and practices—has a huge impact on our happiness and success."
ADAM GRANT, AUTHOR & PSYCHOLOGIST[1]

SOMETIMES THE NEWS reports can make one wonder and ask, "What is going on? "Do people care how their actions impact others?" Business leaders and politicians are violating their power, making deals and playing with financial statements to fill their wallets at the detriment of organizations and employees, and sometimes still ride away with their golden parachutes. People once revered in high regard and viewed as pillars of strength are committing fraud, extramarital affairs and various forms of harassments and abuse. School teachers and administrators are violating the innocence of children in institutions established to be safe havens for the kids while they are apart from their parents. What is the issue? How can leaders do such abominable things and act as if nothing happened? They have no values for themselves and no regard for others. There is a demise of core values, and everyone is suffering.

These issues plaguing the world require a change in direction, and this change must be a new or renewed commitment to core values that enable everyone to thrive. The world needs leaders with strong, upright morals and positive values who stand for what they believe at any cost. There is a need for more leaders like the late Nelson Mandela, who went to prison standing for what he thought was right, and would not denounce his beliefs to attain his freedom.[2] "[He] knew who he was at his core. He knew his values, and his leadership reflected those values."

Values are vital in shaping one's personal life as well as the organizational culture as they represent what people believe, care about, and stand for.[3]

53

A value is an enduring belief that a specific mode of conduct or end-state of existence is personally or socially preferable to an opposite or converse mode of conduct or end-state of existence. A value system is an enduring organization of beliefs concerning preferable modes of conduct or end-states of existence along a continuum of relative importance.[4]

Once the values are accepted, they become the "standards of importance" and facilitate the decision-making process. As values are psychological and internal to an individual, organizations do not technically have values.[5] However, since organizations comprise people, their collective values shape the corporate values; therefore, there needs to be a commonality among people in order for the organization to grow. Without shared values, an organization will not thrive. For these reasons, leaders play a crucial role in shaping the values of the organization and ensuring the organization is intentional about creating and promoting values for a win-win-win culture for employees, customers, stakeholders and investors. To this end, leaders take time for:

- Self-Discovery and Authenticity
- Understanding the Team's Need and Values
- Core Values Statement Development
- Promotion of Core Values
- Value through Appreciation

Self-Discovery and Authenticity

Leaders have a critical role in developing, promoting and protecting the values of the organization[6] as they live out their own personal values. Therefore, exceptional leaders need to be authentic in understanding their personal values and stand by them in their interactions with others.[7] They need to know who they are and their personal direction.

They understand that values development and self-discovery begin with one's childhood (e.g., obedience and punishment) and continue throughout the various stages toward adulthood; it's a lifelong process.[8] Their continuously evolving values set the stage for how they navigate through life, defining their needs and behaviors. Their values influence decisions and priorities and become their personal "'bottom line.'"[9]

The leaders' values give them the needed confidence to be themselves, contribute ideas, make decisions, and not mimic others and their views.[10] The leaders' values are so much a part of them that even during a crisis, they do not compromise them but allow these challenges to strengthen them.[11] Leaders know their "voice"—their inner selves.[12] They know what is important to them and their leadership philosophy.

Leaders can discover or validate their values and understand the values of their team with the clarify values exercises (Exhibit 6.1):

Exhibit 6.1

Clarify Values
1. Examine past experiences to identify the values used to make choices and decisions.
2. Answer the question, "What is your leadership philosophy?"
3. Articulate the values that guide your current decisions, priorities, and actions.
4. Find your own words for talking about what is important to you.
5. Discuss values in various recruitment, hiring, and onboarding experiences.
6. Help others articulate why they do what they do and what they care about.
7. Provide opportunities for people to talk about their values with others on the team.
8. Build consensus around values, principles, and standards.
9. Ensure people are adhering to the values and standards they have developed as a team.

Adapted from Kouzes and Posner (2012), 69.

As the leaders understand and define their values, they have to assess their alignment with the organization's values.[13] If they determine there is a misalignment between their personal and organizational values, leaders can attempt to transform the organization's values, adapt to the organization's values, or those leaders may need to leave. Otherwise, there will be conflict. Change is required, and the leader has to stay true to self.

Understanding the Team's Needs and Values

In order for organizations to succeed, they need a culture where leaders take the time to understand employees—what they need and value.[14] Leaders can no longer expect employees to accept unsuitable work conditions because of their need for employment.[15] Leaders must understand and appreciate the needs of their people and create a positive and flexible work environment.

Similar to a leader's journey to value creation, employees' values are also shaped as early as childhood.[16] All life experiences help determine who they are and what is important to them. Through the work of Abraham Maslow, there is an understanding of the five levels of needs, which influence behaviors and are an intricate part of everyone's lives.[17] These needs include physiological needs (e.g., food, water), safety and security (e.g., protection, consistency, stability), social needs (e.g., a sense of belonging, social acceptance), esteem (e.g., respect from others), and self-actualization (e.g., achieving goals). There are also interpersonal needs: inclusion (relationships), control (need to be in charge, influence); and affection (warmth, open and honest communication). All these needs help leaders understand what drives people; and therefore, what shapes their values.

Besides needs, leaders also have to embrace the fact that there are primary generations of employees in the workforce contributing to the diverse needs and values in the organization:[18]

Generation	Birth Year
Baby Boomers	1946 – 1964
Generation X-ers	1965 – 1977
Millennials/Generation Y-ers	1978 – 1995

Their work-life values are provided in Table 6.1. As leaders acknowledge and understand the team's diverse needs and values, they might be overwhelmed, wondering how to address these varying needs or establish core values. However, taking the time to understand the differences and similarities of these groups will give them the clarity they need to lead and help them shape the policies that appeal to the team members individually and collectively, enabling a healthy work environment. In addition, they will have a better appreciation of the team differences, which can facilitate the effective and efficient resolution of team problems.

Core Values Statement Development

"Core values are the ideals and principles that lie at the heart of an organization and guide all of its behaviors. They are the foundation upon which all strategies, processes, decisions, and actions rest."[19] Core values address what is most important to the organization relative to its employees, customers, operations, and what needs to be protected no matter the cost.[20] Therefore, the core values statement needs to support the

Table 6.1

		Work-Life Values of the Generations	
	Life Style	**Work Style**	**Benefits**
Veterans **Born before 1946**	• Patriotic • Religious • Joins organizations (Rotary clubs, etc.) • Volunteers • Conservative about family & politics	• Accepts hierarchical management • Standard operating procedures • Traditional roles • Loyal to one organization • Keeps work & family separate • Enjoys troubleshooting • Makes good mentors	• Part-time, including PTO • Financial seminars • Long-term care insurance • EAP support • Wellness programs • Eldercare resources & referrals • Legal services • Technology support
Baby Boomers **Born 1946–1964**	• Committed to community and military • Takes family vacations • Enjoys baseball, football • Active in politics (chooses parents' political party) • Supports children's activities • Affected by 1960s social standards • Divorce common	• Loyal to employers • Supports traditional roles for women • Enjoys leadership roles • Accepts long hours • Joins business organizations • Climbs career ladder • Makes good mentors	• Flexible schedules • Career development • Health & fitness programs • Financial planning • Legal services • Eldercare resources and referrals • Technology training • Management training
Generation X **Born 1965–1977**	• Manages life with technology • Single-parent homes common • Latchkey kids • Aware of drug culture • No time for volunteering • Focused on family and children • Prefers skiing, hiking, cycling	• Casual dress • Dual-income couples • Enjoys workforce diversity • Trusts new economy, not pensions • Highly skilled in IT • Expects to be part of mission • Wants training/recognition • Committed to programs, not organization • Values personal knowledge and coaching	• Telecommuting, PTO • Childcare resources & referrals • Adoption subsidies • Free-agent careers • Mentoring & management training • College subsidies • Health & fitness programs • Parenting seminars, EAP

Extracted from Byrd (2008), 11.

Table 6.1 (continued)

	Work-Life Values of the Generations		
	Life Style	**Work Style**	**Benefits**
Millennials/Generation Y Born 1978–1995	• Experienced in and committed to technology, e.g., text messaging • Often prefers friends to family • Foreign travel for social causes • Postpones marriage • Gets news from TV, Internet, blogs • Active in politics • Has Facebook (et al.) profile	• Values environment, ecology, and diversity • Entrepreneurial at young age • Prefers teamwork • Multi-tasking & competitive • Wants constant feedback and quick success • Confident about skills • Wants leading-edge training • Blogging for career change	• Flex-time and PTO • College subsidies • Management training / mentoring by leaders • Health & fitness programs • Self-branding for careers • Recognition & awards • Pet resources

Extracted from Byrd (2008), 11.

vision and mission of the organization and may differ from those of other organizations.[21]

Developing the core values statement needs to be a collaborative effort, including leaders and employees at all levels[22] to increase the probability of success with everyone—leaders and followers—living them out. There are two steps in defining the core values:[23]

1. Identify the foundational principles that will determine the organization's relationships with employees, customers, partners, suppliers, and other stakeholders.
2. Describe the core values relative to how people will live them.

The team needs to have passionate discussions until everyone agrees. The team should not be concerned about impressing others with the list, but determine what will resonate with all personnel in developing their attitudes and actions while remaining realistic and practical.[24] They have to understand the significance and complexity of core values development and the hard work required.[25] Therefore, they need to take the appropriate amount of time to develop the core values and ensure they truly represent the personality of the company.

The core values statement may consist of three to ten values,[26] covering such topics as quality, productivity, customer service, employee safety, diversity, community relations, and environmental awareness.[27] The three most common areas of focus among successful organizations are customer focus, continuous improvements, and employee empowerment (Table 6.2).[28]

Table 6.2

Values and Beliefs	
Value	**Fundamental Beliefs**
Customer Focus (Serving the Customer)	• Business is a chain of suppliers and customers (e.g., teamwork inside and outside the organization) • The customer is the purpose of the work (e.g., exceed expectations, build trusting relationships) • Success comes from valuing the voice of the customer (e.g., listening and acting on their feedback, including them in the product design) • Support core values: service, humility, and integrity
Continuous Improvements (Finding a Better Way)	• Know the facts (e.g., data gathering and sharing) • Analyze, understand, learn and benchmark with other companies—collect the right data and ask the right questions • Know there is always a better way (e.g., no complacency with success) • Keep trying for perfection; however, one will never achieve it (e.g., celebrate progress and raise the bar) • Support core values: honesty, humility, and hard work
Employee Empowerment (Working Together)	• Employees are people (e.g., look beyond headcount and their functions and see the people) • People are basically good (e.g., believe people want to do good work, equip them and trust them) • Bureaucracy kills initiative (e.g., let go of the hierarchy and give responsibility to the people) • The manager's job is to provide training, tools, and support (e.g. equip the team, reward success, and allow failure) • Support core values: humility and hard work

Extracted from Snyder, Dowd, and Houghton (1994), 153–95.

These values emphasize the significance of people (e.g., customers and employees) and the quality of the organization regardless of industry, product, or service.[29] While some people may consider this focus to be common sense, the stated values, the meaning of the values, and the importance of values go far beyond,[30] and the employees at all levels are to have the behaviors and actions to support them.

When developing and assessing their values, organizations need to ensure the values have balance, viability, alignment, and authenticity.[31] All the values have to be weighted properly compared to each other, and employees need to be confident the values are achievable within the organizational culture. There also has to be synchronization of individual, team, and corporate values, and the values genuinely need to represent the people and the organization.

Promotion of Core Values

Leaders have a crucial role in ensuring the values are stated clearly and understood by all parties as the team executes and makes decisions based on these values or expectations.[32] Leaders have to look for ways to incorporate them into everyday life.[33] For example, the core values need to be in writing for all employees to know what they are.[34] They can be published on framed posters, websites, and pocket-sized cards.[35] Leaders can discuss core values at meetings, team-building activities, celebrations of significant contract wins, and performance metrics. This repetitive communication integrates the core values into everything people think, do, and say.[36] Leaders can reinforce core values in the performance evaluations, reward programs, recruitment, and training initiatives. Leader also promote the core values when using them to guide the selection of strategic partnerships, ensuring alignment of values and not just performance.[37]

There can be times when unwritten values seem to overrule stated values.[38] If negative behavior and values are becoming prevalent and the preferred method of operation, leaders need to address quickly as these actions are sending a wrong message to the employees. There may also be cases where there is a conflict of values. For example, a value of achieving high profit margins may cause some leaders to mistreat or exploit employees, going against other values. These conflicting values require action. If leaders do not address them, the negative values become the norm, causing confusion of the written and unwritten value system and creating an unhealthy, toxic work environment. Therefore, leaders have to be courageous, disciplined, and determined as they fulfill their role; just having vision and values is not enough.[39] "Good intentions are laudable, but they have no material value if they are not carried out." Core values need to be ingrained in the employees so they can state them with no hesitation,[40] and live them out.

Value through Appreciation

The appreciation of people—employees, customers, stakeholders—is one core value leaders instill in all employees as people are invaluable to any organization. Without them, there are no products or services; and therefore, no customers, no revenue, and no profits. Organizations can show people value by having culture statements relative to people, recruitment efforts that only select people who fit in the culture, training that promotes people-value, and leadership initiatives that encourage people-value.[41]

Financial compensation (e.g., salaries, bonuses, benefits, promotions) is a way of rewarding employees; however, despite financial rewards, studies show that 66% of employees (76% of millennials) will quit their jobs because of a lack of appreciation.[42] They need and want something more than money, and this "more" is other forms of appreciation[43] as some people may not know they are valued until they walk out the door. Therefore, wise leaders care for and appreciate their employees. They determine creative ways to express this care and appreciation while creating a climate for others to share their gratitude. However, as not all employees are the same, having unique personalities, backgrounds, and needs, employees require unique expressions of appreciation.[44]

Gary Chapman and Paul White provide suggestions for workplace appreciation in their book, *The 5 Languages of Appreciation in the Workplace*. These five languages include words of affirmation, quality time, acts of service, tangible gifts, and physical touch (Table 6.3).[45]

While these acts of appreciation are self-explanatory, they require time. Leaders and staff have to take the time to know each other, their partners, suppliers, and customers. While people can complete questionnaires to identify their appreciation languages, leaders and teammates can glean an understanding by observing people's behavior—what they say, do, complain about, and request—as people tend to speak their own personal language in their interactions with others. For example, a person who encourages others may have the words of affirmation as his appreciation language. A person who is coordinating lunches with people may appreciate quality time. The key to appreciation effectiveness is responding to people in their language and not one's own. These appreciation languages can help guide leaders and fellow teammates on how to personalize the appreciation, which may not always require money.

In a #MeToo world and the proliferation of reports about inappropriate behavior, the appreciation languages of physical touch and words of affirmation may be challenging. Dr. Chapman and Dr. White share that they do not promote physical touch as it was previously assessed as one of the least significant means of

Table 6.3

Five Languages of Appreciation in the Workplace	
Appreciation Language	**Examples**
Words of Affirmation (Positive words that uniquely affirm a characteristic of an individual)	Sincere written notes, or one-on-one or public recognition for accomplishments.
Quality Time (Focused attention)	Active listening, personal chat (in-person or phone call), lunch, team outing or retreat.
Acts of Service (Helping others)	Volunteering to help with a project or problem, accomplishing the tasks "their way," bring in food if the staff is working long hours.
Tangible Gifts (Thoughtful gifts unique to the receiver; something they would appreciate)	Gifts specific for the person within the organization's guidelines—tickets, gift cards, time off (not a mug).
Physical Touch (A mutually appropriate gesture)	Gestures such as a firm handshake, high five, pat on the back. (Note: These gestures depend on the culture, person, situation, corporate guidelines, and the perception of the recipient. This appreciation language is not promoted in the workplace.)

Adapted from Chapman and White (2012), 45–52, 59–62, 73–77, 83–91, and 93–102.

appreciation and there were limited gestures viewed as appropriate in the workplace. Expressions of appreciation depend on the national and organizational culture, the person, situation, corporate guidelines, and the recipient's perception. For example, some employees may appreciate a high five or a pat on the back when celebrating a job well done. A hug may be appropriate for a person dealing with a loss or other personal tragedy. Complimenting a new haircut or style of dress may also be suitable depending on the person.

Sometimes not saying or doing something can be just as awkward and challenging when trying to create a healthy culture. For example, if John always wears jeans and sport shoes to work and then he starts a new preppy look, saying something about it would be welcomed, whereas not acknowledging the change may cause him to feel nonexistent. If Sara, a long-haired brunette, comes to work with a short red hair style, how would she feel if people do a double take but not say anything? Everything boils down to the person and perception.[46] How does the recipient feel? If in doubt, err on the side of caution, following corporate guidelines and the black-and-white forms of appreciation.

The primary objective is to take the time to appreciate each other genuinely and appropriately. Encouraging employees through appreciation enables the organization to improve employee retention, attendance, productivity, and customer satisfaction.[47] There is also a better corporate culture with improved relationships between leaders, employees, and colleagues.

Conclusion

Creating a thriving culture based on shared values requires a heart-to-heart discussion with self. Leaders and employees have to reassess their personal core values to see if they need to be revamped according to moral and ethical standards to influence the right core values in the organization and the next generation of leaders. As the organization develops and communicates its shared core values in spoken and written forms, they have to ensure leaders and employees know them, and are continuously reminded of them. Most importantly, leaders and employees have to personify the core values, hold each other accountable, value and appreciate each other as they walk in unity to fulfill the vision and mission of the organization, yielding lasting results.

Chapter 6 - The Values ACT

Assess Your Attitude & Actions

Based on the content of this chapter, please assess your leadership responsibility and influence in developing and living the core values, including valuing people.

Chapter 6 Assessment	1	2	3	4	5
Rating Scale: 1=Strongly Disagree 2=Disagree 3=Neutral 4=Agree 5=Strongly Agree					
My organizational culture promotes living out the written core values, including valuing and appreciating people.					
I know the core values and I live by them. I also value people and express appreciation to them.					
I promote and facilitate the understanding of and adherence to the core values among my staff, peers, superiors, stakeholders, and others. I also encourage them to value and express appreciation to others.					

Commit to Personal & Organizational Changes

Based on what you know and have read regarding core values and appreciation and your personal assessment above, what are you committing to improve for yourself, your staff, peers, superiors, stakeholders, or others?

Commitment	Commitment Date	Target Date
1.		
2.		
3.		

Transform Your Thoughts

*"Wise are those who learn that the
bottom line doesn't always have to be their top priority."*
William Arthur Ward, Author[48]

"When your values are clear to you, making decisions becomes easier."
Roy E. Disney, Businessman[49]

*"I have learned that as long as I hold fast to my
beliefs and values—and follow my own moral compass—then
the only expectations I need to live up to are my own."*
Michelle Obama, First Lady and Author[50]

*"Just as your car runs more smoothly and requires less energy to go faster and
farther when the wheels are in perfect alignment, you perform better when your
thoughts, feelings, emotions, goals, and values are in balance."*
Brian Tracy, Author[51]

*"Feeling gratitude and not expressing it is like
wrapping a present and not giving it."*
William Arthur Ward, Author[52]

"All of us thrive in an atmosphere of appreciation."
Gary Chapman and Paul White, Authors[53]

Leaders ACT to THRIVE!

CHAPTER 7

Ethics that Thrive

"The time is always right to do the right thing."
DR. MARTIN LUTHER KING, JR., CHRISTIAN MINISTER & ACTIVIST[1]

JASON WAS A well-accomplished, educated business professional. As he worked on his projects, his manager asked him to move resources from one project to another to allow enough funding. Leslie's team was working on their strategic plans and struggling for competitive information. Executives asked the team to gather information by calling competitors, pretending to be prospective customers. They also shared IDs for accessing purchased industry research. Erin did not like Jay, one of her employees, and created a lot of challenges to block his success; he eventually resigned.

What is common about these situations? Are they ethical violations? What should employees do in these cases? Do they have the freedom to challenge authority? Did the leaders or the followers assess the requests or actions to be unethical or illegal?

After the business scandals of WorldCom, Enron, and several others during that time period (early 2000's), Laurence J. Kirshbaum, former chairman and CEO of AOL Time Warner Book Group, asked John Maxwell to write a book on business ethics.[2] John argues ethics need not be qualified with the word, "business." A person is ethical, or he is not, regardless of area—personal or professional. There is no in between. Likewise, for the context of this chapter, ethics is ethics. This chapter covers principles of ethics with no distinction in organizational ethics, business ethics, or any other type of ethics. So, what is ethics?

> Ethics is concerned with the kinds of values and morals an individual or society finds desirable or appropriate… Ethics is concerned with the virtuousness of individuals and their motives. Ethical theory provides a system of rules

or principles that guide [people] in making decisions about what is right or wrong and good or bad in a particular situation. It provides a basis for understanding what it means to be a morally decent human being.[3]

Ethics provides the foundation for all people in every organization (e.g., business, government, church, school, community) to do the right thing in every situation, or have the foundational principles to objectively and ethically address the shades of gray with inner peace about the right action to take or decision to make. As people have different understandings of ethics, a common understanding of right and wrong is needed to have effective working relationships, which can help to bring some objectivity and ethical focus to challenging situations.[4]

Maintaining an ethical standard throughout an organization is everybody's business at every level. Every member from top to bottom has to be engaged. "Ethics is one topic that begins and ends with people."[5] While some persons may make the mistake of thinking ethics is just common sense, there is no room for ignorance for the leader. He needs to have the information necessary to make ethical decisions, give direction to promote and not hinder ethical behavior, and intelligently, respectfully, and humbly question data and people.

While there needs to be an environment of trust,[6] it cannot be at the expense of accountability. Everyone in the organization is responsible and accountable for the ethical climate of the organization, and the leader has to be the standard, showing the way. Therefore, the goal of this chapter is to provide a framework and checklist for establishing and maintaining this much needed ethical environment where everyone works together for the betterment of the employees, customers, shareholders and stakeholders. Ethics cannot be a one-time event but integrated with other processes and training for specific disciplines (e.g., marketing, human resources management, finance, and accounting).

Leaders and business professionals in their fields have to follow organizational and professional codes of conduct, understanding that they have a legal and moral obligation to adhere to these ethical standards. They also have to know that titles do not matter. Wrong is wrong, and right is right. Rank and position should never override ethics; therefore, leaders are responsible for:

- Model of Ethics
- Courageous, Ethical Culture
- Comprehensive Ethics Program
- Code of Ethics
- Ongoing Ethics Training
- Personal and Mutual Accountability

Model of Ethics

Leaders need to build a personal leadership brand (PLB) for being and doing the right thing, and understanding the impact their leadership has on the organization.[7] Honest responses to key questions can help to shape one's character or brand.[8] For example, the leader honestly assesses and answers these questions: "Are you the same in your private and public life? How do you perform your daily obligations when no one is looking? Are you accountable to others?"

James Kouzes and Barry Posner in their book, *The Leadership Challenge*, encourage leaders to "model the way"[9] through one's behavior to earn the respect and gain the commitment and results expected in others. Leaders especially need to "model the way" in promoting and maintaining an ethical culture with everyone in the organization engaged and committed. Leaders lead by example and set the standard, starting with their character, which is "what [they] do when [they] think no one is watching… Character defines who [they] are and forms the basis of [their] leadership. Without it, leadership is impossible; with it, leadership can flourish."[10]

One's character and ethical mindset will be especially challenging during the "defining moments" of having to choose between right and right options.[11] They are also challenged by ethical blind spots, which can have a negative impact on the leader and others dependent on his decisions and actions.[12] Therefore, the leader has to work on changing himself by addressing the misalignment between what he "wants" to do versus what he "should" do.[13] One may think he will behave as one should; however, when the decision or situation arises, one does what he or she wants to do. Later, when one reflects on the situation, he may conclude he behaved appropriately. Strategic tactics of thinking through the ethical challenges before they arise can help the "should self" to win over the "want self," and consulting with a trusted friend or counselor can be helpful.[14]

As leaders strive to model ethics for others to follow, there are five ethical leadership principles leaders should demonstrate:[15]

1. Respect others. Leaders respect and appreciate employees for who they are, their values, goals, and dreams and not just value the team as the means for which the leader achieves his personal goals. In getting to know and understand each other, the leader can integrate the employees' values and goals into the team's values and goals.
2. Serve others. Leaders follow the altruism theory of ethics to prioritize the needs of others ahead of their own. Leaders serve their employees as they empower, mentor, listen and nurture them in achieving goals. They also commit to serving the community and making things better for the less fortunate.
3. Act justly. The leaders treat all people with equity. They give each employee

"an equal share or opportunity, according to individual need, person's rights, and individual effort…, societal contribution…, merit, or performance."[16] When necessary, leaders make exceptions for moral, ethical reasons. Leaders live by the Golden Rule, treating people the way one wishes to be treated and with understanding and respect of their cultural differences, which may warrant a different communication or action.[17]
4. Be honest and authentic.[18] Leaders are to be honest and authentic, open and transparent with discernment in what to share, not to share, and when to share. Leaders do not over promise, misrepresent information, or avoid taking accountability for their actions.
5. Promote team spirit and community. Leaders take the time to understand the purpose, desires, and goals of their followers without pushing their will on others. The leader is also concerned about the public interest.

Courageous, Ethical Culture

Leaders and followers have a significant impact on the success of the organization and the ethical climate in the workplace.[19] Leaders establish the vision, mission, values, structure, and ethics of the company and also manage the success of the programs with rewards and disciplinary actions to promote the desired behavior within the organization. As the leaders and followers are in partnership to achieve the mutually desired goals of the organization ethically, the ideal is for leaders to include followers in decisions affecting their welfare.[20] This involvement enables the followers (i.e., the leaders' partners) to provide their leaders a high level of support with the freedom to challenge their behavior and actions,[21] creating a win-win-win for all.

Employees are empowered to ask questions and address concerns without fear of retaliation.[22] They are inspired to take responsibility for their success and the organization's success, going the extra mile to serve the leader and the organization. They are free to confront leaders' inappropriate behavior or disagree with process or strategy, and be an active participant in the organization's transformation. There is also mutual accountability to achieve goals and maintain an ethical organization.

Comprehensive Ethics Program

When empowering employees to make wise, independent decisions, having a comprehensive, effective ethics program is essential to support the decision-making process and provide a clear understanding that unethical practices are not acceptable.[23] This program should include the formal and informal cultural factors that contribute to the ethical climate of the organization.[24] The formal components include a code of ethics, mission statements, core values, structure, evaluations, and rewards while the informal factors comprise traditions, behaviors, language, and stories. Other elements of a good program include:[25]

1. Corporate awareness of legal and ethical policies throughout the organization so that all employees understand what to do as some violations may be due to not knowing the facts or the laws.
2. The code of ethics is practical, well-written, and easy to use. It is a living document translated into different languages and updated periodically to add or delete topics, or revise content for relevance. Having one ethics document can also be more user friendly versus keeping content separate based on function or category (e.g., purchasing, marketing, sales, and safety).
3. There is a variety of options for addressing confidential verbal and written complaints—ethics office, hotline, email, company mail, etc.
4. Confidentiality is required in any program as some employees are fearful of retaliation from their superiors; and therefore, do not report ethical issues.
5. The program needs to be action-oriented. If employees submit issues, the ethics department needs to investigate and act accordingly.
6. The program promotes fairness and equality at all levels. The organization treats everyone the same. Just as an individual contributor or employee will be punished for incorrect reporting, a manager, director or higher-level leader has similar or greater consequences.
7. The program promotes resolution among the individuals when possible versus solely depending on the ethics office. They do not have to wait for others to act; they can help push things forward, holding people accountable for resolution without retaliation. Individuals can seek coaching through the process as needed.

Code of Ethics

Code of ethics is a critical component of the ethics program, providing the guidelines for employees to know right and wrong behavior.[26] Organizations ensure it is clearly written and correctly used; otherwise, it can contribute to a host of challenges.[27] Employees in the various disciplines (e.g., marketing, finance) of the same company may use different ethical reasoning, guidelines, and subclimates. There can also be various interpretations of the code of ethics relative to content and intent.[28] This ambiguity creates challenges for the employees; however, these issues can be combatted by ensuring compliance of the code of ethics.[29]

1. Communicate the standards and principles of the desired behaviors to live by relative to the industry, profession, or organization.

2. Establish general or specific pragmatic principles of employee behavior relative to ethical dilemmas like acceptance of gifts or treatment of customers.
3. Maintain one document for the whole organization with consistent information.[30]
4. Include the following topics, which will vary depending on the country as different rules and behaviors will apply:[31]
    - Standards of Conduct
    - Adherence to the Law
    - Employees
    - Customers
    - Shareholders
    - Business Partners
    - Community Involvement
    - Public Activities
    - The Environment
    - Innovation
    - Competition
    - Business Integrity
    - Conflicts of Interests
    - Compliance (e.g., Monitoring, Reporting)

The code of ethics can also include guidelines to help employee apply the principles. For example, there are steps (used at Texas Instruments) that can help employees objectively assess if their proposed actions or decisions are ethical:[32]

1. Assess the legality of the behavior or decision.
2. Assess if the act or decision complies with corporate values.
3. Evaluate how one may feel (good or bad) if completed or not doing it.
4. Assess the media's potential response.
5. Do not do it if you know it is wrong.
6. When in doubt, ask questions.
7. Be persistent until all questions are answered. Consult with colleagues, legal, HR, and the ethics department.

Ongoing Ethics Training

Formal ethics training can equip business professionals with the information and tools required to recognize, evaluate, and resolve ethical challenges accurately.[33] This training is a critical component of the socialization process and has to be ongoing to maintain an ethical culture.[34] Essential elements of an effective ethics training program include:

1. Training needs to be unique to the organization, industry, or profession.[35] Ethical challenges in academics (e.g., grading, tenure) will differ from those in healthcare (e.g., patient privacy, malpractice). Employees need the skill to identify ethical challenges, which may not be obvious. Also, leaders and training providers need to have a keen understanding of the informal values and messages floating in the workplace that impact the actual climate and

values of the organization.[36]
2. There is sufficient time for interaction and discussion.[37] Training developers allocate significant time for group discussions (large or small), analyzing and resolving case studies, debating and addressing questions. Continued discussions can also occur post-class, leveraging technology (e.g., the internet, collaboration tools).
3. Allowing class participants to share examples can also help to reinforce and supplement the training. This interaction will allow the attendees to teach each other with personal situations and help resolve each other's problems.
4. The training includes a holistic approach by integrating ethics with other organizational programs and training initiatives (e.g., sales meetings, leadership training, and conflict management).
5. The training program includes behavioral ethics.[38] This training will help address the psychological steps causing even a good person to take part in ethically questionable activities that are misaligned with one's personal ethics and values.[39] This additional component of the training will enable attendees to acknowledge their blind spots and fight the internal war between their actual and desired behaviors.
6. Continuous ethical training and promotion can be achieved by providing tools (e.g., videos) of ethical situations employees can relate to[40] and are accessible at their leisure but with deadlines to ensure completion. Mandatory in-person or live, virtual training should also be conducted periodically or as needed.

Personal and Mutual Accountability

Leaders ensure ethical practices are second nature in every discipline (e.g., marketing, finance, and HR) as they fully train all personnel, reminding them of the ethical standards and practices that are to guide every thought, communication, and action. No exceptions. Employees have to have practical knowledge of these ethical standards to ask the right questions and hold each other accountable. They do not have to be experts, but know enough to protect the company and themselves, seeking the proper help and guidance from the experts when needed. Having ethical practices by function consolidated in one document can help to facilitate this accountability.

Conclusion

A strong ethical position is a competitive advantage for an organization[41] and the leaders are responsible for promoting and maintaining this healthy, ethical climate.[42] They prioritize ethics above deadlines and results for a "morally fit" organization.[43] The leaders plan strategically for the organization's ethical success, starting at the recruitment of employees and throughout their tenure in the company. While the organization may not be perfect, all personnel make every effort to determine the best ethical decisions and actions with support from their leadership team who has equipped and empowered them with an ethical, collaborative culture, training, and tools (e.g., code of ethics) to be courageously ethical,[44] enabling them to enjoy a peaceful night's sleep.

Chapter 7 - The Ethics ACT

Assess Your Attitude & Actions

Based on the content of this chapter, please assess your ethical behavior and influence in the organization.

Chapter 7 Assessment	1	2	3	4	5
Rating Scale: 1=Strongly Disagree 2=Disagree 3=Neutral 4=Agree 5=Strongly Agree					
My organizational culture promotes and requires the execution of ethical principles among all leaders and employees at all levels.					
I am ethical and model ethical behavior among my staff, peers, superiors, and stakeholders throughout the organization.					
I promote ethical practices and behaviors in the workplace among my staff, peers, superiors, and stakeholders, requiring mutual accountability to ethical standards.					

Commit to Personal & Organizational Changes

Based on what you know and have read regarding ethics and the results of your personal assessment above, what are you committing to improve for yourself, your staff, peers, superiors, stakeholders, or others?

Commitment	Commitment Date	Target Date
1.		
2.		
3.		

Transform Your Thoughts

*"Ethics is knowing the difference between
what you have a right to do and what is right to do."*
Potter Stewart, U.S. Supreme Court Justice Judge[45]

*"If you're guided by a spirit of transparency, it forces you to operate
with a spirit of ethics. Success comes from simplifying complex issues,
address problems head on, be truthful and transparent. If you open
yourself up to scrutiny, it forces you to a higher standard. I believe
you should deliver on your promise. Promise responsibly."*
Rodney Davis, Politician[46]

"Integrity has no need of rules."
Albert Camus, Philosopher[47]

*"Integrity is telling myself the truth.
And honesty is telling the truth to other people."*
Spencer Johnson, Author[48]

*"Many persons have an idea that one cannot be in business and
lead an upright life, whereas the truth is that no one succeeds
in business to any great extent, who misleads or misrepresents."*
John Wanamker, Businessman & Marketer[49]

Leaders ACT to THRIVE!

PART 2
What We Do (Our Performance)

	What We Do (Our Performance)
T	**Teamwork** that Thrives
H	**Holism** with Continuous Learning to Thrive
R	**Responsibility** that Thrives with Results
I	**Innovation** with Intentional Care that Thrives
V	**Vision** with Strategic Execution that Thrives
E	**Empowerment** to Thrive

CHAPTER 8

Teamwork that Thrives

"Unity is strength... when there is teamwork and collaboration, wonderful things can be achieved."
MATTIE STEFANIK, AMERICAN POET[1]

SALLY, A MARKETING manager in the manufacturing industry, was on a conference call with Brenda, a senior sales director, who was preparing for a meeting with a newly acquired customer. On the call, Sally requested some data, which could only come from the operations team who was not on the conference call. When Sally went to the operations manager, Steve, to get the information, Steve said the information was not available and questioned why the sales team needed it, which was not surprising as he was notorious for not sharing information. The team was not happy with Steve's response; therefore, Sally's boss went directly to Steve with the same request. He retrieved the information immediately; however, Sally's boss did not confront Steve on this issue; everyone moved on as if nothing had happened. What was the problem? Why did Steve not cooperate with Sally? Why did it take a higher-level manager to get the information? If Steve's team is notorious for not sharing information, why has Sally's management team not worked to resolve the issues?

In a non-profit organization, John, a multi-talented leader, full of energy and passion for his customer service role, excelled as the leader of his department. However, one challenge was his lousy attitude and its negative impact on the team. His attitude was so bad at one leadership team meeting, resulting in a fellow team member immediately contacting the boss afterward regarding John's behavior as this was his second outburst at the leadership meetings. Besides this behavior in meetings, John also would not communicate with his boss (e.g., not sharing requested information). Several times the boss scheduled meetings with him to discuss the issues. During the first meeting, John denied anything was wrong. On another occasion, he questioned the leader as if she was making things up. And on the third meeting, he said he forgot about the planned meeting. Given John's poor behavior and team spirit, his boss had no choice but to follow proper procedures to remove him from the team as his attitude and actions were detrimental to maintaining a friendly work environment and ultimately overall team success.

These stories highlight that teamwork requires more than an organizational chart and talented people in position. Leaders have to work at creating highly effective teams, dealing with conflicts in personalities and processes, and resolving other challenges that are hindering the team's success. As the workforce increasingly becomes virtual, teamwork and team effectiveness will be more challenging for leaders to manage. Team members may be domestic or global, working from home, client site or other places of choice, and not have a regular work tour or set of hours.[2] Essentially, the workforce will consist more of transient business professionals with the flexibility to work whenever, wherever, and however they desire, using technology to reach the world. Therefore, agility, flexibility, innovation, and speed are critical to the success of the team and organization.

The changing demographics will also affect the team dynamics for in the US alone, there is a significant increase in employees over the age of 40, more women entering the workforce,[3] and millennials are the largest working group.[4] Organizations are moving transactional job functions to countries with lower costs while a more substantial amount of complex functions are retained in the US.[5] Globalization, mobility, and hyperconnectivity are also affecting the workforce, along with other technologies (e.g., the cloud, collaboration tools).[6] Workplace behaviors are also changing with the prevalence of social media. All these shifts are contributing to changes in how teams communicate and perform their individual and collective jobs.

Just as it takes work to make a house a home, leaders have to combat all these internal and external forces to turn an organizational chart into a highly effective team that thrives. There is the semblance of a team on the organizational chart (i.e., on paper); however, the establishment of an effective team will require much work in the following areas:
- Team Selection
- Team Development
- Team Communication
- Team Cohesiveness
- Team Collaboration
- Mutual Accountability
- Conflict Management and Resolution
- Team-Building Activities

Team Selection

As leaders strive to fulfill the assigned mission, they strategically determine the team makeup with clearly defined roles and responsibilities. This team needs to comprise a diverse group of people with the commitment and passion to follow the leader in fulfilling the mission. Otherwise, homogeneous teams think and act alike; and therefore, do not yield the best results. While they can achieve monumental goals, the limited team diversity will hinder their performance.

Leaders address this need for team diversity by ensuring the team demographics mirror the markets it serves, and including people who zig where others zag, having a variety of skills, backgrounds, and experiences. Leaders assess the team's strengths and weaknesses to determine the best way to fill the gaps, understanding that everyone on the team does not have to perform all functions for team effectiveness. However, at least two people or more need to have the needed skills, so that there is never a challenge in achieving team goals because of a lack of team capability. As the team members work together, they will value this diversity, knowing they each have a role to play in the team's success. No position is better than the other. They all humbly fulfill their roles for the good of the team and the people they serve.

Team Development

As a team forms and new employees join the team, leaders determine creative ways to enable the team to gel, working effectively and efficiently well together. The team also grows and unites as a team as they progress through the five stages of team development: forming, storming, norming, performing, and adjoining (Table 8.1):[7]

Table 8.1

Five Stages of Team Development	
Stage	**Description**
Forming	Orientation, breaking the ice
Storming	Conflict and disagreement
Norming	Establishment of order and cohesion
Performing	Cooperation, problem solving
Adjourning	Task completion

Extracted from Daft (2015), 301.

This team development process takes time, and everyone should expect to go through these stages. In addition, the leader has to guide the team through these stages in a way that maintains a healthy culture; establishing team charters and norms can aid in team development and effectiveness.

Team Communication

Effective communication is critical to the success of any relationship. It is especially crucial in a flexible, virtual work environment.[8] In the workplace, leaders have to communicate, communicate, and communicate with their team members. Likewise, team members have to communicate with their fellow teammates and upper management. There is no reason for team members to not know what their fellow team members are doing and how all the pieces fit together. Therefore, the leader has to promote and facilitate mutually open and honest sharing of information, knowledge and resources.

Leaders and team members alike have to be astute in using communication tools, knowing when to instant message, text, email, call, or schedule a meeting. They are also digitally savvy when communicating with the younger generation of workers.[9] When managing or leading geographically dispersed team members, they know when to show up for in- person or video conference meetings.[10]

Everyone has to also be careful with their communication style and word choices as they can unintentionally offend or alienate team members.[11] Cultural differences, information overload, filtered communication, and personal communication barriers (e.g., defensiveness) can also hinder communication and team effectiveness. Therefore, team members have to go back to basics with active listening, simplified communications, and sensitivity to others, seeking and applying feedback to overcome any team communication challenges.

Team Cohesiveness

Team cohesiveness is the degree to which team members feel a sense of belonging to the team—they are drawn to each other and want to remain part of the team.[12] High-leveled cohesive teams are committed; they attend meetings and are pleased when the team reaches its goals. Key factors that facilitate team cohesiveness are provided in Table 8.2.

Leaders can influence team cohesiveness in these areas as they develop and lead the team by modeling the desired behaviors. They select diverse team members who not only have the needed skills and experiences, but who also have the desired character and shared values for team cohesiveness and effectiveness. Leaders ensure unity and harmony are always maintained at all costs for the team to succeed. They work with team members who are a hindrance to this team cohesiveness, coaching them through the necessary steps to achieve the desired behavior. If they cannot follow the norms of

Table 8.2

Key Factors for Team Cohesiveness	
Factors	**Explanation**
Team Interaction	Team members get to know each other through frequent interaction. Their involvement and exchange with each other facilitate commitment and feeling like a team.
Shared Goals	Team members have a sense of purpose and direction regarding something important and pertinent. They know where they are going and are participating in the journey to get there.
Team Attraction	Team members are attracted to each other through shared values and attitudes. They enjoy being with each other.
Competition	Competition promotes cohesiveness as the team endeavors to win.
Team Success	Similar to competition, success also has a way of pulling the team together. Team members feel good about themselves and the team, promoting strong team commitment.

Adapted from Daft (2015), 302–3.

the team, they cannot be a part of the team regardless of their skills and contributions. They may leave through a transition to a new team, resignation or termination.

While team cohesiveness takes time and hard work, there are many benefits. Team members enjoy high team morale, having a warm, friendly team environment, pleasant conversations, team participation in decision-making and other activities, team commitment, loyalty, and overall improved employee satisfaction. They also energize each other and achieve higher levels of productivity, creativity, and team performance.

No matter how valuable team cohesiveness is, the team has to be cautious and mitigate the risk of groupthink wherein employees go along with the team and not share relevant, opposing views that could enable the team to make better, informed decisions.[13] These members value consensus and getting along more than being objective in making the right decisions. Such thinking can be costly. For example, the 1986 Challenger space shutter disaster was due to team members not sharing safety concerns for the sake of consensus. Leaders have to determine how to properly balance and minimize this potential risk while enjoying the benefits of team cohesiveness.

Team Collaboration

Leaders and employees alike understand and proactively work towards team collaboration, realizing the whole is better than the sum of its parts, and working together is a distinguishing trait of successful organizations. Collaboration works horizontally between employees and teammates throughout the company, and it works vertically between leaders and followers wherein employees share their views and what they need to achieve their goals. There are mutual trust and accountability between leaders, employees, and departments.

When assigning projects or tasks to team members, leaders instill this spirit of collaboration. While there is a project leader, all team members know they are expected to collaborate with each other, and no one holds back ideas or information that could facilitate the project's success. They contribute to the project as co-owners of the project. Therefore, project leaders always acknowledge people for their contributions, and team leaders consistently look for ways to promote and recognize team collaboration.

Organizations can also facilitate collaboration by using collaboration platforms to help teams connect and engage with each other, sharing information whenever and wherever with any device.[14] These platforms can enable the storing, archiving, tagging, searching, or retrieving of information. This sharing of information builds trust while allowing leaders and team members to recognize and appreciate their peers and build strong networks, whereas nonparticipation will be noticeable, creating challenges for the individual and the organization.

HP Labs demonstrated a high-level of trust and collaboration during their efforts to build a lab in Bangalore. At the onset of this project, an Indian director determined she would be a more effective asset to the team by staying in Palo Alto, California.[15] She could promote and advocate for the new lab at the US headquarters as she had worked in the US for many years and knew how to lobby and sell the business case for the lab. A scientist in India had a wealth of local knowledge, understanding the government, academia, business practices, and the associated challenges of building an HP lab in India. He was truly qualified to be the liaison between the Bangalore Lab and Indian environment. In addition, HP assigned an American executive to India to bridge the gaps between India and HPs global business units. Together, the team could accomplish the team's mission. They leveraged their knowledge, skills, and experiences to create a winning solution for HP and contributed to HP's global knowledge for others to learn. If they had not strategically placed the right leaders in the right place and did not have the trust and comradery to work together, results would have been limited as witnessed by Shiseido, a Japanese cosmetic firm. They did not have the cosmopolitan leaders to bridge the cultural and business gaps. They entered the global perfumery industry but did not add any value in achieving global goals as the knowledge stayed hostage in France. While all collaboration engagements may not be this complex, collaboration is truly better than a siloed team.[16]

Mutual Accountability

All persons on the team are mutually accountable in achieving the team's mission and goals.[17] Leaders inspire and promote this accountability, providing the team with clearly defined goals and objectives they can realize, and the tools and resources to execute. Leaders also ensure the work environment is conducive for the individuals to do their jobs successfully, removing any challenges or hindrances impeding their performance. They encourage and enable team members in their commitment to each other and other cross-functional or matrix-managed teams in achieving results, ensuring they do their jobs on time with excellence, accuracy and integrity. The team may go beyond the call of duty when necessary, even when the leader may not have initially communicated all information or requirements. Leaders can assess this mutual accountability not only by results but through team effectiveness evaluations and 360-degree assessments.[18]

Conflict Management and Resolution

Successful teams welcome and promote healthy discussions and conflict to determine the right solutions. Just like marriage, in business, if two people agree with each other on everything, one person is not needed. Conflict is good for the team even though it can require much work to resolve. Leaders have to own it and help the team work towards a resolution, and the team members have to be open and honest in sharing their views. If they ignore the conflict, they weaken the culture as the avoidance demonstrates that people are afraid to speak or they are going along to get along (e.g., groupthink). This conflict avoidance also hinders team effectiveness, preventing the constructive conflict and discussion of multiple views that could contribute to a better solution.[19]

To resolve the conflict, team members have to understand that conflict resolution is about the topic, solving a problem and not making it personal. The goal of the discussion is to reach a win-win-win solution that is best for all people. Therefore, if inappropriate language or personal attacks enter the conversation, leaders have to address and stop the behavior immediately. Otherwise, this conflict will not only hinder team performance, but will also cause other intra-team issues (e.g., disagreements, communication challenges, distrust, and decreased team spirit).[20] Without a doubt, leaders have to own and manage conflict and must lead the team to a collaborative, win-win-win resolution.

Team-Building Activities

As leaders strive to enhance team effectiveness and performance, they will occasionally host team-building activities, enabling team members to build trust and comradery. In most cases, team building may comprise games or activities, requiring employees to work together, depend on and learn more about each other—critical for team success. All team members may not embrace these activities as they require them to get outside of their comfort zones, but they are encouraged to try.

Besides the fun and game, leaders also can enhance their team building efforts by recognizing and rewarding team members for a job well done (individually or collectively) and supporting them where needed. Leaders along with their team members can use their words to build each other up with encouragement, constructive feedback, and input that will help them achieve goals and become their best. As the team members grow together and bond as a team, they develop a genuine care and concern for each other and will make personal sacrifices for teammates to succeed or support them in other areas of life (personal or professional). What team member would not welcome this kind of team building?

Conclusion

Teamwork requires work. It goes beyond the organizational chart, hosting meetings, delegating responsibilities, completing projects by any means necessary. It requires skill, discernment, and tenacity to create a thriving team that works well together to achieve results. Leaders have the primary role in attaining team effectiveness and efficiency, and building team comradery wherein everyone on the team is each other's cheerleader and support system. They celebrate successes and work through challenges whether work-related or personal, learning from each other's successes, failures, and risk-taking experiences.

The team has a genuine care and concern for each other with no hypocrisy. While members hold each other accountable, they do not play the blame game when they do not achieve desired results. As they strive to become a cohesive team, they understand they are all part of a bigger, corporate team, and may sometime need to forgo or reprioritize individual projects or goals for the good of the larger team and the ultimate team victory for the win-win-win where everyone thrives.

Chapter 8 - The Teamwork ACT

Assess Your Attitude & Actions

Based on the content of this chapter, please assess your leadership and influence in promoting an effective team culture.

Chapter 8 Assessment	1	2	3	4	5
Rating Scale: 1=Strongly Disagree 2=Disagree 3=Neutral 4=Agree 5=Strongly Agree					
My organizational culture promotes and enables effective teamwork.					
I am a team player and leader. I intentionally contribute my part to the team. I communicate and collaborate with colleagues to enable a cohesive, effective team.					
I promote teamwork in the workplace among my staff, peers, superiors, and all stakeholders, providing the environment and opportunities for everyone to collaborate and work well together.					

Commit to Personal & Organizational Changes

Based on what you know and have read regarding teamwork, and your personal assessment above, what are you committing to improve for yourself, staff, peers, superiors, stakeholders, or others?

Commitment	Commitment Date	Target Date
1.		
2.		
3.		

Transform Your Thoughts

"None of us is as smart as all of us."
Ken Blanchard, Author and Management Expert[21]

"Alone, we can do so little; together we can do so much."
Helen Keller, Author, Political Activist, and Lecturer[22]

"If you can laugh together, you can work together."
Robert Orben, Writer[23]

Leaders ACT to THRIVE!

CHAPTER 9

Holism with Continuous Learning to Thrive

"Those people who develop the ability to continuously acquire new and better forms of knowledge that they can apply to their work and to their lives will be the movers and shakers in our society for the indefinite future."
BRIAN TRACY, AUTHOR, SPEAKER, AND CONSULTANT[1]

BARBARA WAS AN exceptionally astute business professional, managing her career like a business, always developing and enhancing her skills to maintain her marketability in the workplace. As an engineer, working closely with internal clients, Barbara assessed she needed to get closer to the customer and balance her technical skills with business skills. Therefore, she started pursuing an MBA, which opened the door for her to move into a marketing role, an opportunity provided during a departmental restructure. After four months on the new job, Ray, the vice president, executed another reorganization, requiring all employees to reapply for their jobs as he was striving to have more people on the team with a variety of skills to include experiences outside of the IT industry (i.e., his definition of diversity).

While Barbara kept her job during this departmental transition, she took the VP's vision and comments to heart and realized she needed to complete her MBA as soon as possible and set new career goals. Instead of planning to retire with her existing company, which was her original goal and over 25 years away, she concluded she needed to explore external opportunities to gain this "diversity" of skills to maintain her marketability. In her quest for new experiences and skills, she sometimes faced the challenge of not being able to use all of her skills in her 9-to-5 positions, and therefore sought opportunities within the community to use and grow her skills. Sometimes, opportunities discussed in the job descriptions and interviews differed from reality, not allowing her to realize fully her dream and career aspirations.

Barbara's challenges in the workplace demonstrate a "knowing-doing gap," wherein employees have knowledge and skill but may not have the opportunity to use them for the betterment of the organization and personal growth.[2] Holism is lacking in the workplace. In 1996, there were over 1,700 business books. A 2019 search on "business books" at Amazon.com resulted in over 50,000 business books found, a significant increase in over a twenty-year period.[3] According to Statista 2019 reports, in 2018, organizations spent $366.2 B (USD) globally on corporate training[4] while they consumed $274.86 B (USD) on global management consulting.[5] There is apparently a wealth of knowledge available to any business manager or leader wanting to succeed and make wise decisions while leveraging the skills, talents, and experiences employees like Barbara bring to the workplace.

These challenges Barbara and other professionals experience are partly due to having leaders like Ray who in their effort to meet a business goal, have not taken the time to learn and value the wealth of knowledge at their disposal. Leaders are responsible for creating a healthy culture of holism with continuous learning so that organizations and employees thrive with win-win-win opportunities that enable employees to reach their goals as they partner with leaders to realize and exceed corporate expectations. In addition, leaders thrive and they open the door to their learning from employees and vice versa. Leaders can create this holism in a continuous learning culture as they promote:

- Executive Attitude and Mindset Transformation
- Strategic, Continuous Learning Organization
- Honest, Open Communication on Career Goals
- Win-Win-Win Performance Agreements and Appraisals
- Leadership Modeling (Knowledge and Execution)
- Succession Planning

Executive Attitude and Mindset Transformation

Leaders play a critical role in helping the organization realize its goals. However, they cannot do it without the cooperation of their employees who not only work for monetary compensation but who are seeking to use, enhance, and grow marketable skills, which may be more important than the financial rewards. Too often, employees cannot use their knowledge and skills, hindering their ability to excel, and the organization also suffers. Therefore, leaders have to change their paradigm of looking at their role as delegating projects and having a pool of resources to use. Their mindset transformation has to include learning how to utilize effectively their resources for the good of the team individually and collectively. Before the delegation of responsibilities, projects, and assignments, the wise leaders will take time to uncover these hidden treasures (e.g., knowledge and skills), and understand employees' career goals, interests, and professional needs to create effective partnerships with their followers, providing opportunities to leverage their skills toward mutual goals and edification.[6]

When employees see a genuine care and concern for their career and have opportunities to act on their passion, they are inspired in such that they will spend personal time and corporate resources to realize organizational and personal goals. They will deliver their best, going beyond the call of duty to fulfill the mission. They have a passion and excitement of getting the job done, and do not have to seek opportunities outside the organization (e.g., part-time jobs, or community projects) for personal fulfillment. They have a one-stop-shop opportunity to learn, grow, and innovate beyond everyone's imagination, having fun on the journey. The employee wins by enhancing skills and experiences, and developing new skills and experiences while the organization gains products, services, processes and operational efficiencies that delight internal and external customers, and retain loyal employees who enjoy their jobs. There is value in this executive mindset transformation that enables a win-win-win—everyone thrives!

Strategic, Continuous Learning Organization

Leaders are also diligent in creating a learning organization. Yes, employees have a responsibility for their personal growth; however, leaders ensure employees can meet the day-to-day functions with vision for the future, requiring continuous learning and skills development. Leaders and employees have to be ready for skill shortages, global competition, technological innovations, and the inevitable need for change and adaptation to change.[7]

Brainpower or knowledge is the organization's most valuable corporate asset and competitive differentiator.[8] Therefore, leaders are to have the strategic foresight to look ahead into the future and determine the skills and knowledge necessary to be ready for future opportunities. Leaders can gain and maintain this brainpower through intellectual stimulation and individual consideration,[9] giving employees challenging opportunities to promote their personal growth and boost their confidence while ensuring alignment of the employees' long-term goals with the organization's current and future needs.

In the book and movie, *Hidden Figures*, based on a true story, Dorothy Vaughan, a mathematician and supervisor at NASA in the mid-1950s, assessed that she and her team of human computers needed to understand Fortran, a computer programming language, and the IBM computer, to enable a successful career.[10] Otherwise, they eventually would lose their jobs. She inspired and prepared her team, taking classes to learn the language, and they were ready when the opportunity knocked. No one could deny them the work; they had gained the knowledge and were valuable to the organization during its time of need.

When leaders are not prepared, and do not equip their team, they may have to execute drastic measures to achieve goals. For example, senior management gave Susan an additional responsibility, requiring a new skill her existing staff did not have, and she had to build this function with no additional headcount. To fulfill this additional responsibility, Susan had to restructure her organization, merge departments, and layoff people to free up resources to hire people with the desired skill. What if Susan and her senior management had been more strategic in previous years and started preparing their staff for the new needed capability? They would have boosted morale and promoted a healthy work environment while providing opportunities for loyal employees to continue to grow their skills and avoid such a significant disruption in their lives. They would have eliminated or minimized the effects of the layoff, including costs associated with employee separation packages and recruitment. All the shakeup was because there was no strategic foresight and continuous learning at all levels of management and the employee base.

Leaders have to create a learning organization that is performance-based and aligned with business objectives.[11] Everyone knows the significance of learning—it is everybody's business with everyone at every level committed with the right attitude to learn new skills and gain knowledge.

> To go from a non-learning to a learning organization requires a significant transformation, similar to the metamorphosis from a caterpillar to butterfly. The caterpillar undergoes some messy transitions on its way to becoming a butterfly. The raw protoplasm in the cocoon re-forms (re-engineering, restructuring, refocusing) to become a butterfly, a beautiful creature with the power to fly in all directions, to flow with the wind or find safety from it.[12]

Likewise, an organization's culture, vision, strategies, and structure must go through a metamorphosis—a dramatic change, equally focusing on learning and development versus only on work and productivity.

In this learning transformation, there are a variety of learning and development methods to use, including employees teaching and learning from each other through all experiences (e.g., successes, failures, and risk-taking). Learning and development can also come from formal training, mentoring, reverse mentoring, coaching, and other forms of learning geared towards the individual, including self-development. It will require strategic foresight, thinking globally and locally,[13] learning and executing new technologies and forms of communications (e.g., social media).[14]

Continuous learning may also require leaders and executives to let go of activities they may want to do or feel more comfortable doing so their staff may grow and develop to achieve their learning and career goals, strengthening the team. Essentially, leaders should strive to become replaceable versus feeling threatened by their employees. This learning takes time with growing pains. However, there is a return on the investment (ROI) as the individual and company-at-large will improve marketability and competitive differentiation.[15]

Honest, Open Communication on Career Goals

Steve worked for a large organization wherein employees freely shared their career goals with their managers, who willingly helped them achieve their goals to include movement to another department within the company. In return, there were loyalty and longevity in the organization, and managers could strategize with the employees based on the needs of the business. For example, during one reorganization, Steve had several employees interested in a career change, which he would not hinder but knew he needed to keep some of his staff to achieve business goals. Therefore, he proactively reached out to some employees and encouraged them to stay with him during the transition, promising that he would help them move to a new job when they were ready.

Mary had an unpleasant experience as she worked in an organization wherein she could not talk freely about her career goals or apply for new opportunities without challenges. Therefore, she did not stay with the organization long. She had to move on to achieve career goals even though there were opportunities she could have considered internally if not hindered by her management. Her departure, like other resignations, created a corporate expense as the organization had to recruit and train new employees.

Employees should be able to discuss their career goals honestly and not just say what they think their bosses want to hear. These conversations can open the door for brainstorming assignments and new ideas that mutually benefit the employee and organization. This open and honest communication can help the employee achieve goals while assisting the leader to be strategic and timely in grooming and preparing the team for a future void, ensuring the team does not skip a beat in fulfilling responsibilities and achieving results. What a win-win-win!

Win-Win-Win Performance Agreements and Appraisals

Leaders and employees may also reconsider the purpose of appraisals. While performance evaluations provide a forum for employees and their managers to discuss their goals and have follow-up discussions to assess progress, in reality, this exchange does not occur as designed or desired.[16] A win-win-win approach for addressing the appraisal from the perspective of the employee's vision may work better in enabling personal mastery. The employee and manager will discuss the employee's desired goals for the next year and future years, strengths and weaknesses impacting achievement, and needs from the company and manager to achieve results. The boss can use this information to align the employee's goals with those of the company for a win-win-win. Based on the mutual goals, the manager monitors progress to determine if there are any warning signs that require his intervention, addressing the need for employee's skills development and possible mentoring inside and outside of the department or company. The manager also encourages the employee to mentor others to succeed him eventually while allowing employees to take on higher levels of responsibilities and ownership. Although some organizations and leaders may not fully embrace this appraisal process, any leader-follower relationship can benefit from a mutual goals discussion.

Leadership Modeling (Knowledge and Execution)

Having the right leaders in position who model the desired culture, know their role and how to execute is critical to the success of the organization in achieving its goals. They are to be the examples for aspiring leaders who are watching them to determine what to do to succeed. While all employees may not desire a leadership role and reality says there are not enough positions at the top for everyone to hold leadership or executive titles, they still can possess leadership skills that can be leveraged for the good of the company and their personal growth. Therefore, the right leaders need to be in place to lead by example and have coaching and mentoring attitudes and abilities to grow future leaders at every level of the organization.

Unfortunately, sometimes corporations send the wrong message to employees by their leadership selection. While there are some exceptional, qualified, and deserving leaders in leadership positions, there are also unqualified leaders in positions for title only, or who were given the job because of who they are or who they know. There are some who have worked hard for the title, being the expert in their industry, technical, or functional area; however, they may lack the character, people skills or business acumen to succeed in leadership. There are others who have great leadership (i.e., character and competence) but do not get the chance to lead for lack of exposure or perhaps not fitting a certain mold. This leadership challenge and perpetual recruitment of the same leaders create a lose-lose-lose for the organization, leadership team, employees, and ultimately the customer.

If the organization is to thrive, it has to move the right people into leadership roles through effective recruitment and succession planning, training and development, staff realignment, and possibly other organizational changes specific for the company.

When the right people are in leadership, the company and employees grow with no one questioning why or how the leaders achieved their leadership positions. They have the knowledge, training, and execution abilities to lead. They train others as they lead by example, coach and mentor employees to thrive. Everyone wins!

Succession Planning

The thriving organization has a leadership bench strength for sustainability—people with character, knowledge, skill and experience for promotion to leadership when the need arises. Leaders have a fair, ethical, and inclusive process for recruiting and training future leaders, mirroring the global diversity of the company's customers.[17] As some leaders dominate the culture, having a significant influence on values and success criteria, they also select and promote people who look like them; therefore, organizations must go the extra mile to ensure equity among women and minority groups to facilitate their success and rise to leadership positions.[18] Addressing diversity in the recruitment, training, succession planning, and leadership selection processes can help the organization overcome this challenge as there will be diverse leaders in place to influence the culture and leadership demographics.

Some leaders may have other blind spots blocking their view of potential leaders in the organization; therefore, besides addressing diversity, the organization can uncover these hidden jewels by allowing people to volunteer for the succession planning program and other leadership recruitment initiatives. For example, as assistant vice president of events planning for a non-profit organization, Brenda created an organizational structure with leadership positions and opened the door for any interested person to apply for the jobs. This process allowed her to learn a lot about the talents and skills of the people inside and outside the organization, including John who had earned an advanced degree in events management; he was the perfect candidate for the events management and logistics team leadership role. He was efficient in negotiating contracts with venues, and he introduced alternative ways of setting up events for everyone's comfort and enjoyment. These talents might have remained hidden if Brenda had not given everyone a chance to apply.

As part of the succession planning process, leaders and the training and development team have to ensure the leadership candidates understand the role of leadership and be able to fulfill the leadership responsibilities. They have to know they cannot keep doing the same thing as before to be successful.[19] Besides performing their job function well (technical skill), they have to manage people (people skills), and set vision and strategy (conceptual skill).[20] As they advance to higher levels, conceptual skills will be more critical while technical ability becomes less critical; mastering people skills is a requirement at all levels (Exhibit 9.1).

Exhibit 9.1

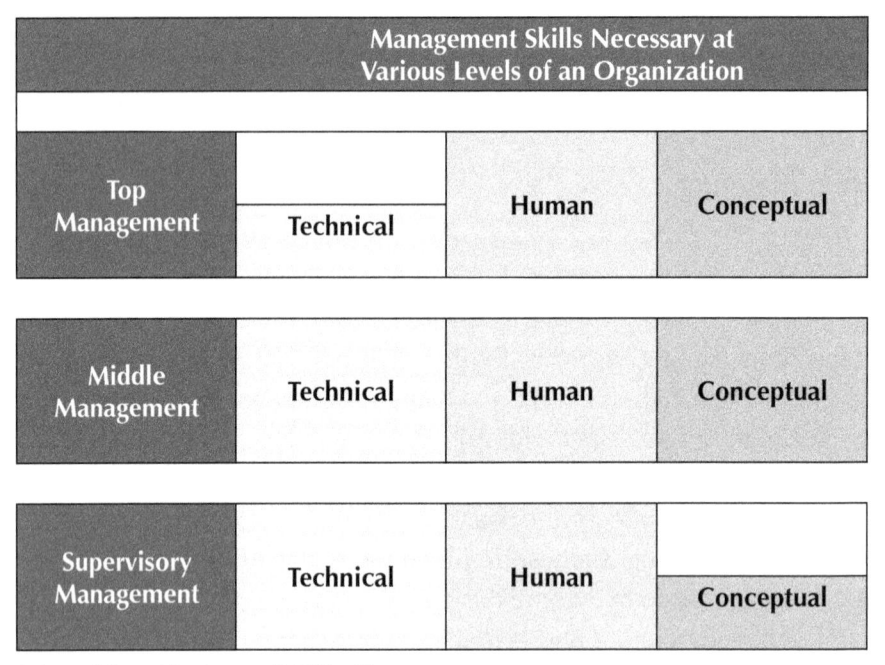

	Management Skills Necessary at Various Levels of an Organization		
Top Management	Technical	Human	Conceptual
Middle Management	Technical	Human	Conceptual
Supervisory Management	Technical	Human	Conceptual

Adapted from Northouse (2013), 45.

Along with revisions to the succession planning program to ensure equity and qualified leaders, organizations need to have solutions for promoting and rewarding hardworking individuals who are experts in their discipline or industry but do not have the skill or desire to lead or manage people. Also, employees at all levels must understand that it is acceptable and expected for leaders to not have more technical skills than their followers to succeed. The leaders focus has to be on their leadership and people skills along with enough industry and functional knowledge to understand and see strategically the big picture to provide the vision, strategy, execution and inspiration for the team to succeed collectively and individually.

Conclusion

Creating a holistic, continuous learning culture does not mean leaders settle or compromise corporate needs for the benefit of the employees. Quite the opposite. By developing employees and allowing them to pursue their passion for the good of the organization, everyone wins.

Leaders have the privileged role to establish an environment that can realize a higher return on investment (ROI) beyond what they could imagine with improved marketability and competitive differentiation, creating a win-win-win solution for the employees, organization, and customers to thrive. The ROI includes improved morale and longevity, and everyone is adaptable to change internally and externally, having the confidence, skills, and knowledge to meet the needs of the business while growing new capabilities for future success. Therefore, leaders and employees must continuously exercise strategic foresight, openly discuss what they see on the horizon, and act on the information (i.e., plan and execute). However, despite these efforts, there will be times when the organization or an employee needs to end the partnership (e.g., transition to another position, resignation, termination). Even this change can be a win-win-win and not a surprise to anyone because of the open and honest communication in working towards mutual goals with everyone growing and learning through the process.

Chapter 9 - The Holism ACT

Assess Your Attitude & Actions

Based on the content of this chapter, please assess your leadership and influence in promoting a holistic and continuous learning culture.

Chapter 9 Assessment	1	2	3	4	5
Rating Scale: 1=Strongly Disagree 2=Disagree 3=Neutral 4=Agree 5=Strongly Agree					
My organizational culture enables holism with continuous learning for all employees at all levels.					
I am using all my skills and experiences in my role, and share important information and lessons learned with others. I am proactive about my continuous learning for my current job and career success.					
I promote holism and continuous learning in the workplace among my staff, peers, superiors, and all stakeholders, providing opportunities for others to grow and achieve career goals and enhance the organization's intellectual capital.					

Commit to Personal & Organizational Changes

Based on what you know and have read regarding holism with continuous learning and your personal assessment above, what are you committing to improve for yourself, your staff, peers, superiors, stakeholders, or others?

Commitment	Commitment Date	Target Date
1.		
2.		
3.		

Transform Your Thoughts

*"Never become so much of an expert that you stop gaining expertise.
View life as a continuous learning experience."*
Denis Waitley, Speaker, Writer, and Consultant[21]

*"Anyone who stops learning is old, whether at twenty or eighty.
Anyone who keeps learning stays young."*
Henry Ford, Founder of the Ford Motor Company[22]

*"It's essential to keep moving, learning and evolving
for as long as you're here and this world keeps spinning."*
Rasheed Ogunlaru, Life Coach, Speaker, and Author[23]

*"We need to internalize this idea of excellence.
Not many folks spend a lot of time trying to be excellent."*
President Barack Obama[24]

Leaders ACT to THRIVE!

CHAPTER 10

Responsibility that Thrives with Results

"The price of greatness is responsibility."
WINSTON CHURCHILL, FORMER BRITISH PRIME MINISTER & AUTHOR[1]

NO MATTER HOW exceptional the organizational culture—everybody liking each other, everybody getting along, everybody representing the corporate image, and everybody executing well—the organization must achieve results. It has to deliver quality products and services to its customers and performs on its metrics. Are goals or key performance indicators reached or exceeded? Are the employees, customers, and shareholders satisfied? Can the organization go beyond just sustaining? Can it thrive today and in the years to come? These are just a few of the questions responsible leaders ask and answer every day, knowing their decisions and actions impact other people's wellbeing and the organization's success. They know they have to put their best foot forward consistently with responsible followers committed to doing the same to achieve the desired results.

Leaders are responsible for the "what" and the "how" as they lead the organization to succeed and they are accountable to deliver. They inspire others to play well together to win and achieve results—deliver extraordinary products and services that delight customers, keep and grow the customer base and loyal employees, beat the competition, and exceed shareholders' expectations. This need for exceptional results requires responsible actions to thrive, including:

- Executive Commitment and Responsibility to be the Standard
- Mutual Responsibility and Accountability
- Establishment of an Analytical Culture for Fact-Based Decision Making
- Development of Responsible Followers
- Responsible Risk Taking and Successful Failure

- Corporate Social Responsibility
- Execution and Measurement of Results
- Ownership of Decisions and Results

Executive Commitment and Responsibility to be the Standard

Before leaders can build a responsible organization that achieves results, leaders and board members must first get real with themselves to ensure they are up for the challenge of responsibility. They are to be responsible leaders at the core, living and leading the model of leadership, being the outstanding citizens in their home, community, and on the job. They understand that immorality, injustice, unfairness, lying, cheating, stealing, and prejudices do not belong in the organization or any part of their lives. Leaders have to have the character, competence, and discipline of leadership representative of the desired corporate culture and brand. They walk the talk and are the example of leadership other leaders and employees look up to and follow. They are the standard.

Mutual Responsibility and Accountability

Leaders also hold fellow leaders responsible and accountable to the standard. If colleagues lack the qualities of responsible leadership, fellow team members or leaders should confront them lovingly and respectfully, but also with firmness and understanding to promote the responsible attitudes and behaviors necessary for a thriving organization. Any misalignment with no effort or desire to change will require action as organizations can only afford to have leaders in position who behave appropriately. Leaders holding others accountable to the standard are also mindful that people cannot give what they do not have. Therefore, leaders and employees have to have honest assessments and communication to determine if the organization is the right fit and make appropriate decisions. There must be a cultural fit beyond performance. Like kids in school, all personnel are to be rated and rewarded for conduct besides performance.

Establishment of an Analytical Culture for Fact-Based Decision Making

Leaders and followers need the right information to make wise decisions; therefore, leaders have to ensure the correct data is collected for immediate and future use, storing information in databases for easy retrieval, research, and analysis. Leaders enable this action by building an analytical culture where projects and decisions are fact-based.[2] They eliminate guessing games from the equation, and people are free to question and reject projects that do not have supporting data.

The questioning is not to be negative, rude, belittling, or challenging for challenging sake. The goal is to have all bases covered in refining and perfecting the concept or idea for insightful decision making and effective usage of corporate resources. One's intuition, experiences, processes, team input, and other tools can also aid in the decision-making process.[3]

As Davenport, Harris and Morison discuss in their book *Analytics at Work*: *Smarter Decisions, Better Results*, there are seven attributes employees possess in an analytical culture[4]:

1. Look for the facts to be objective and logical.
2. Determine the root cause and look for patterns in the data, asking a series of five why's to get to the root cause.
3. Expect the details for better analytics versus just providing and accepting summaries or averages.
4. Expect and use data versus stories or anecdotes for decision making. As data can be bland, use stories only to add color to this needed data.
5. Appreciate negative data in addition to positive data as it can be just as insightful and useful.
6. Decide and execute based on the information versus allowing power and position to cloud or influence the decision.
7. Know when enough data is enough to avoid paralysis through analysis.

As organizations grow to embrace these behaviors, leaders do not punish people who are learning through the process, but they celebrate the right actions to reinforce expectations.[5] Over time, the behaviors become so ingrained that they are a natural part of the team. Leader are also patient through this organizational transformation that complements other cultural qualities (e.g., ethical, innovative, strategic) while enabling competitive differentiation.

Development of Responsible Followers

Outstanding organizational achievement depends on leaders and followers performing at their exceptional best. This work excellence comprises three essential performance factors—focus, capability, and will, and the interdependencies and interactions of the three (Table 10.1).[6] Any change in any of these three factors may affect the others. The ideal situation is when all three elements harmonize.

With these factors in mind, leaders can help create a culture that optimizes performance through engagement and motivation. Leaders can involve employees in the development of a shared vision, which enhances their focus. As capability and the will depend on the Maslow's Hierarchy of Needs, once the lower-level needs

Table 10.1

The Performance System	
Performance Factors	**Explanation**
Focus	Focus represents a clear definition and understanding of the performance proposed; focus is associated with questions such as what…?; how…?; who…?; where…?; when…?; and why…?
Capability	Capability represents the ability to transform into reality the performance defined in focus; capability is associated with such diverse areas as skills, budgets, tools, and physical assets.
Will	Will represents the strength of intent to act to carry out the performance defined in focus; will is associated with attitudes, emotions, beliefs, and mindsets.

Adapted from Smith and Sharma (2002), 767–68.

(i.e., physiological, safety, and social belonging) are addressed, employees will seek esteem and self-actuation, which can be influenced by intrinsic and extrinsic motivation. Extrinsic motivation is key to capability development, which also affects the will while intrinsic motivation influences the will directly. Although people are different and are motivated differently, they all need to see the big picture and enjoy satisfaction with completion and achievement; therefore, leaders should provide opportunities for employees to succeed and be recognized.[7] Leaders should also invest the time to learn more about their staff and work life to determine the best way to inspire and spark their inner motivation, touching their minds and hearts.[8]

Organizations can also influence employees in the areas of focus, capability, and will through meetings and action learning. Meetings provide the social setting for employees to interact with each other and enable employees to feel a sense of purpose and competence while motivating them to achieve the vision through action. Therefore, leaders are to conduct meetings such that the tone and words improve interactions, enabling people to be more open to sharing who they are while engaged and attentive to others' needs.

Action learning is also key to performance, providing a safe environment that builds on where people are versus where people should be with no connections between the two.[9] There is a personal reflection on what needs to be accomplished, what helps, what hinders, and what one will do to progress forward. While there is also group questioning that contributes to information sharing and results, the responsibility to act lies with the individual.

Responsible Risk Taking and Successful Failure

Successful organizations embrace responsible risk taking for founders and co-founders of any existing company took some level of risk and sometimes experienced failures along the way before succeeding. The results are relative to the level of risk and the strategy to get there.[10] When organizations decide to change, they are also embarking upon some level of risk. These changes or risks can be in the form of new products and services, expansion in new markets, reorganization, new processes, and resource management.

Novartis, a Swiss international pharmaceutical company, experienced 90% of product failures during the onset of their R&D process; however, their failure rate decreased to 30% seven to ten years later. Vasella, the former CEO, stated, "There is no way around it; we succeed less often than we fail… You have to be willing to learn how you minimize the impact of failure."[11] In addition, while leaders need to know the stakeholders and their views, they have to be free to make the right decision without feeling pressured to go with the flow or be politically correct. They have to have the guts to do what they believe is best for the short and long term.[12]

Leaders also have to remove the fear of punishment while rewarding desired behaviors to encourage employees to use newly gained knowledge.[13] Any level of fear can be detrimental to organizational results as employees may be concerned with losing their jobs, self-esteem, or future. These fearful employees will then dwell on past successes and keep doing the same old thing with no growth, repeating problems and mistakes, creating a "knowledge-doing gap."[14] Removing fear frees them to be their best and do their best to achieve their best for the good of the organization and themselves.

Corporate Social Responsibility

Without a doubt, leaders must ensure shareholder value, market leadership, employee and customer satisfaction, regulatory and legal compliance, along with all the other requirements for running a thriving business. Beyond these responsibilities, there is an increasing need to achieve the associated business goals aligned with corporate social responsibility (CSR).[15] Organizations committed to CSR "consider the interests of society by taking responsibility for the impact of their activities on customers, suppliers, employees, and stakeholders as well as the environment."[16] They have an inspiring, understandable, and quantitative CSR commitment[17] that is integrated into their business plan and strategies, including relative goals and measurements.[18] While organizations include the CSR commitment and accomplishment in the annual report or standalone CSR report, shareholders may eventually require a balance sheet with the triple bottom line—people, profits, and planet.[19] Also, CSR is becoming a deciding factor for recruiting and retaining top talent, especially among Millennials (a.k.a., Generation Y) and Generation 2020 (a.k.a., Generation Z).[20]

Execution and Measurement for Results

Once leaders make fact-based decisions, people need to execute.[21] Knowing is not enough; the team has to perform. Their acting on this knowledge will enable the achievement of results and continuous learning.[22] They also have to measure what they execute to add to the data gathering for future use.

The team tracks the metrics essential to the business, which will be part of the data analytics.[23] They compare these analytics with other relative data to see what is changing and to what extent these changes are taking place (e.g., revenue increased by 10% compared to last month). The team presents the metrics as a ratio or rate, affecting the way people act or respond to the metrics. People are able to understand the metrics and effectively talk about them.

These measurements need to include accounting and experimental metrics. The accounting metrics include the success factors like revenue and sales to enable the company to reach financial goals, has the cash flow to pay the bills, and keeps shareholders or investors happy. The experimental metrics include testing new products or strategies and having metrics that determine the decisions. For example, if the marketing campaign increases sales by 20% within the two-month period, the campaign will be extended.

These metrics will provide a level of accountability and discipline to keep everyone focused on the goal, gaining the necessary knowledge to know when to stay the course or change direction. Having data analytics and decision tools will not guarantee perfection or success. However, they will improve the possibilities of success and better results.[24]

Ownership of Decisions and Results

Responsibility also requires leaders to own their decisions and outcomes. They own the good and the bad, learning from the successes and the failures. They own it when there is a win, giving credit to whom credit is due. They also own the poor decisions when things do not go so well. When leaders own their mistakes and discuss their lessons learned, employees are free to do the same to enhance mutual learning and improve future decisions and results—a win for all.

Conclusion

Building a culture of responsibility requires leaders to understand the difference responsibility versus compliance has on the organizational culture.[25] Compliance to rules and regulations can help mitigate risks, promote fairness, or reinforce specific behaviors.[26] However, this compliance can cause the culture to be rigid and lead to an environment of blame, accusations, fear, and mistrust.[27] Therefore, effective leaders have to balance compliance with responsibility to mitigate the possibilities of a negative culture.

The responsible leader also promotes a culture of shared values, encouraging commitment and responsibility to the mission for the good of all.[28] There is a spirit of trust, hope, purpose, encouragement, and mutual growth.[29] There is courage versus fear, and people have an emotional attachment to the mission. Leaders model the desired, responsible behavior they want to see in their staff, and they also have accountable leaders at lower levels.[30] They inspire the team with stories that resonate with their heart, soul, and mind.[31] Performance becomes the desired byproduct versus the goal[32] with creative ways to measure success beyond the financials.[33]

Chapter 10 - The Responsibility ACT

Assess Your Attitude & Actions

Based on the content of this chapter, please assess your leadership responsibility and influence in achieving results for the organization to thrive.

Chapter 10 Assessment	1	2	3	4	5
Rating Scale: 1=Strongly Disagree 2=Disagree 3=Neutral 4=Agree 5=Strongly Agree					
My organizational culture enables responsibility and achievement of results among all employees at all levels, collecting relevant data to facilitate an analytical culture and fact-based decisions.					
I am responsible and committed to achieving results so that the organization thrives, making fact-based decisions and collecting relevant data.					
I promote responsibility and achievement of results in the workplace among my staff, peers, superiors, and all stakeholders, enabling everyone to succeed, making fact-based decisions and gathering relevant data for future success.					

Commit to Personal & Organizational Changes

Based on what you know and have read regarding responsibility and results and your personal assessment above, what are you committing to improve for yourself, your staff, peers, superiors, stakeholders, or others?

	Commitment	Commitment Date	Target Date
1.			
2.			
3.			

Transform Your Thoughts

"To thrive, all businesses must focus on the art of self-disruption. Rather than wait for the competition to steal your business, every founder and employee needs to be willing to cannibalize their existing revenue streams in order to create new ones. All disruption starts with introspection."
Jay Samit, Businessman[34]

"Your positive action combined with positive thinking results in success."
Shiv Khera, Author[35]

"Leadership is not a right—it's a responsibility."
John Maxwell, Author & Speaker[36]

"Culture drives great results."
Jack Welch, Author & Business Executive[37]

"However beautiful the strategy, you should occasionally look at the results."
Winston Churchill, Former British Prime Minister & Author[38]

Leaders ACT to THRIVE!

CHAPTER 11

Innovation with Intentional Care that Thrives

"Innovation distinguishes between a leader and a follower."
STEVE JOBS, BUSINESSMAN AND CO-FOUNDER OF APPLE CORPORATION[1]

WHEN PEOPLE SEE a package with the label, "Handle with Care," they deliberately treat it with much attention and caution. Whoever is handling it carefully places it in the car or vehicle for transporting and is particularly cautious about items placed on top of it or around it. The label may even dictate how it should be carried for safe arrival to its destination. When the recipient or owner opens the package, he also proceeds with caution, not wanting to damage the contents. All persons involved understand its value and act accordingly.

Likewise, organizations should also handle innovation with care. So what is care? Care is defined as the "interest, regard or liking… [It is the] close attention, as in doing something well or avoiding harm."[2] When innovating, the entire organization should take great care in creating solutions to solve customers and prospects' known and unknown problems today with foresight for tomorrow. When the interest, the focus is right when the focus is on the people—success will come. When leaders of organizations in the public and private sectors, governments, communities, churches, educational institutions take the time to care, they solve problems for the good of the people. Organizations will enjoy market leadership and profitability while governments and politicians keep their constituents happy, resolving poverty, unemployment, healthcare, and other concerns of the people they serve. There is a win-win-win, and everyone thrives!

Imagine that! Engaged leaders who understand and care for their customers and constituents and are intentional about innovation, creating the vision, culture, and plan to sustain and thrive today and in the years to come. With this caring, innovative mindset and vision, leaders can rightly expect their employees at all levels to be engaged and have the intrapreneurial spirit and mindset for continuous innovation. These leaders will take the time to establish an environment that embraces fresh ideas at all levels. They encourage and reward employees for sharing their thoughts and insights, and for delivering results that exceed expectations with competitive differentiation and wow factor. Leaders can bake this innovation into the organization as they stir up these key ingredients:

- Executive Action and Promotion
- Innovation Strategy
- Commitment to Resource Allocation
- Team Inclusivity and Ingenuity
- No Toleration of Naysayers or Group Thinkers
- Training and Learning
- Customer Empathy and Engagement
- Incentives and Rewards Programs

Executive Action and Promotion

Leaders create and sustain the desired corporate culture.[3] They are passionate about innovation and use their position, authority, and credibility to influence and transform the culture toward consistent innovation. They are not complacent with the status quo and will go beyond what is comfortable, having the vision, motivation, and personal discipline to demonstrate to employees and customers that innovation is woven into the fabric of their being. They personify the innovative culture.

Leaders create alignment between the business strategy and innovation strategy with short-term and long-term goals for market leadership and profitability.[4] They welcome changes and new ideas from people at all levels. They provide the guidance, knowledge, resources, systems, and processes to equip the organization for successful, profitable innovation, creating value for its customers, partners, and suppliers. They are astute in prioritizing initiatives and making the sacrifices and tradeoffs for success. They balance efficiency and innovation; otherwise, no innovation gets done.[5]

Innovation Strategy

All companies, big and small, need to create, document, and communicate their innovation strategy with all employees at all levels.[6] Some organizations choose a "'play-not-to-lose'" strategy (PNTL) wherein they have a keen eye on the market and competition and can make quick decisions. Others may select a "'play-to-win'" (PTW) strategy, determining innovative, competitive differentiation too difficult for others to copy easily or quickly, giving them a market leadership and competitive edge. There are others who may fear innovation and do not innovate, having a play-it-safe mentality, which is the most dangerous strategy of all. The best strategic approach is integrating the PTW and PNTL strategies, creating strategies to support the organization's business model with agreement throughout the organization. According to Michael Schrage, author of The Innovator's Hypothesis, "great strategic visions can inspire great experimentation that neither busts budgets nor defy leadership aspirations. Truly great strategic visions give permission to make faster, better, and [frugal] experiments great. They empower."[7]

Commitment to Resource Allocation

Innovation success depends on the organization's commitment to resources; therefore, persons leading innovation have to allocate sufficient resources and avoid "part-time" status resources.[8] This commitment also includes maintaining resources for innovation even during economic downturns and corporate downsizing. Without resources, there is no consistent flow of ideas for new products, services, and processes, resulting in a loss in market leadership, decreased profits, and product obsoleteness, causing the organization to stay in a rut with a business-as-usual mindset and loss of any competitive edge.

Companies also have to allocate time for innovation. Leaders cannot overwork their people and expect them to be creative. Innovation is a process and mindset that takes time through learning, doing, and failing. Innovation has to be a vital part of the performance objectives and appraisal with mutually agreed upon time allotment for continuous innovation activity, individually and collectively. However, this commitment will require leaders to become more strategic in how they use their total person-hours by assessing and prioritizing projects to achieve results. Evidence shows that this investment of time yields a favorable return as proven by the world's most innovative companies like Google, Amazon, Apple, Microsoft, Samsung, Netflix, IBM, Facebook, Adidas, and many others.[9]

Team Inclusivity and Ingenuity

No one questions the ingenuity of innovation heroes like the Henry Fords, Bill Gates, and Steve Jobs who have engineered solutions that have amazed and transformed lives for the better, creating solutions the world did not know it needed. However, their contributions cause some to believe the myth that only geniuses conceptualize innovations.[10] Not true! There are no lone rangers in innovation. For example, Neil Armstrong is renowned for being the first man on the moon; however, this historical feat was due to the many years of diligent hard work of crew members and over 500,000 NASA employees. Organizations enable innovation through collaboration and partnerships as noted by Guy Kawasaki, author of *Rules for Revolutionaries,* and former Apple employee.[11] He states, "'. . . successful companies are started, and made successful by at least two, and usually more, soulmates. After the fact one person may come to be recognized as the 'innovator,' but it always takes a team of good people to make any venture work.'" Mature innovators have the special sauce or passion to define their "what," and "why" with no egos.

This team ingenuity and innovation effectiveness require executives and all stakeholders with diverse demographics (e.g., age, ethnicity, gender) in all levels and disciplines (e.g., engineering, marketing, finance, and operations) to collaborate.[12] When exploring solutions, the team values and appreciates all ideas and opinions and do not discriminate because of one's position of authority, nationality, personality, or experience. Everyone is free to share their thoughts and ideas.

As executives take part in the process, they have to help lower-level team members understand that executives are just members like everyone else. Designers need not have refined or close-to-final ideas and prototypes before engaging the higher-level executives. Also, executives are not to think they are approving the initiative; they are simply active participants, sharing their views.[13] However, they are to use their position to help unite workgroups that may be the polar opposite of each other (e.g., business and technology personnel)[14] as they create and maintain a spirit of unity within the culture with everyone working together for the common good of others.[15] Customers also are to be an intricate part of the design team, co- developing solutions to meet the market's needs, contributing to group greatness and ingenuity.

No Tolerance for Naysayers and Group Thinkers

As leaders strive to create an innovative culture, there are two groups of people that can work against corporate goals. There are the naysayers who carry negativity with them and thwart the development and refinement of good ideas.[16] And, on the opposite end, there are group thinkers who go along with everything and do not engage in the critical thinking to assess the merit of the concepts to enhance the idea or recommend a hold status for future consideration. Leaders have to teach both groups that change is inevitable to succeed in the dynamic marketplace.

Naysayers and group thinkers have to transform their thinking and acting, understanding that they have an essential role in the organization. They need to commit and contribute their part to the team's successful innovations, sharing all ideas—big or small. They should also question and analyze the information to aid in the assessment and improvement of the concept, and not for the sake of criticism or to show intellectual one-upmanship. The focus is on adding customer and shareholder value, which will enable the right decisions regarding the right innovative solutions for the right time while having other ideas in the pipeline for additional exploration and refinement in the future.

Training and Learning

Innovation is not magical with people dreaming up something that may appear. It is a not a project but a capability that is applicable and repeatable with other products and services,[17] becoming a corporate differentiation that exceeds expectations. Therefore, organizations have to be intentional in creating this innovative differentiation, developing a training and learning environment.[18] Leaders are to formalize the innovation effort in the structure, policies, processes, and systems to ensure learning and innovation are woven into the fabric of the organization.

Learning must be a natural, habitual function of all disciplines (e.g., marketing, operations, and human resources) with opportunities for employees to learn from each other, including successes and failures.[19] Learning initiatives include:

1. Employees stay informed of industry and market trends and new technologies. They know how to define effectively the right customer problems to solve and focus on the win-win-win solution.[20] Determining the right problem is also instrumental in helping the team focus and not go off on different tangents with no purpose, wasting time and resources.
2. They understand the customers and their challenges and use their intuition, pattern recognition skills, idea generation abilities, and empathy to design the right solution.[21]
3. Employees share their findings and key lessons of all projects with fellow employees.[22]
4. Organizations assess, hire, and promote candidates for employment based on their knowledge and ability to facilitate employees and colleagues' learning experience.
5. Leadership, vision, problem-solving, creative thinking, and self-development are also elements of the training process to build these learning competencies in the organization.
6. As employees learn and innovate, leaders ensure there are systems and procedures for capturing and managing ideas for future innovations.[23]
7. Employees at all levels know how to share and receive constructive feedback. They also know there is never a stupid idea or question. In addition, they know how to take a calculated risk (e.g., proposal and approval) for out-of-the-box solutions and learn from failure—critical for innovation health.

Customer Empathy and Engagement

Innovative companies focus on people, understanding their needs and desires, which helps define the right root problems that lead to exceptional opportunities for creating win-win-win solutions.[24] Uncovering customers' needs (spoken and unspoken) requires one to walk in their shoes, knowing more than just surface information, going deeper to understand their feelings and experiences to the point of feeling them also, creating an emotional connection.[25] For example, a person developing a software application for engineers would sit with some engineers, watching their every move, assessing what works well or not working, and observing other challenges that enhance the problem definitions and solutions or become future problems to explore.

Innovative organizations also involve customers in the solution development, including prototyping.[26] Sometimes customers may think they know what they need or want; however, they can best articulate their wishes by playing with a prototype, which is more effective than listing their requirements.[27] Therefore, organizations must be careful in selecting the right participants as they need persons with knowledge, skills and experiences to enable a valuable exchange of information.[28]

When organizations develop requirements without prototyping or customer involvement, they risk giving customers what they may have asked for, but not what they want or need. Also, when customers are engaged, they take ownership of the solution and will partner with the organization in repetitive prototyping, enabling a win-win-win for all.

Incentives and Rewards Programs

Although there is a sense of accomplishment in creating a winning, innovative solution, this journey to success may include roadblocks, misunderstandings, lack of resources, fears, anxieties, and assumptions; and therefore, some leaders and employees may not want to lead or work on innovative projects.[29] To overcome these challenges and promote innovation, exciting incentives and rewards programs are required. As team members are diverse and have different passions, needs, goals, and aspirations, their desired rewards and incentives may vary as no one size fits all.[30] The incentive and rewards program will need to address the four critical elements for motivating participation: compensation or reward for contributions, enthusiasm for the innovation projects, expected recognition, and vision with a well-defined purpose.

Taking time to understand the diversity of the people and their various needs will enable executives and human resources personnel to create the winning rewards and incentives programs that all can embrace. They also have to align the incentive program with the organization's strategies, culture, and systems to ensure retention and longevity of key talent. They will promote risk taking and facilitate a change in the innovation challengers' behaviors (e.g., naysayers and group thinkers). Essentially, the incentive and rewards program has to be designed to encourage the team and enable the achievement of the desired results.

Conclusion

Innovation. Creativity. Differentiation. Disruption. These are the keywords everyone hears in the workplace as organizations strive to delight customers and be the market leaders in their industry. This innovative market leadership as demonstrated by 3M, Google, Apple, Facebook, and many others does not happen overnight. It takes vision, planning, time, and consistent activity to develop this organizational capability with measurable results. Organizations desiring consistent creativity and innovation among employees commit to having leaders who lead by example, aligning words and actions.[31] They are to be the leaders who have a genuine care and vision for improving the lives of others, and strategically make innovation an intricate part of the culture. Innovation becomes an intricate part of day-to-day life with the essential investments in resources—budget, people, time, tools, and rewards.

Chapter 11 - The Innovation ACT

Assess Your Attitude & Actions

Based on the content of this chapter, please assess your leadership and influence in promoting an innovative culture.

Chapter 11 Assessment	1	2	3	4	5
Rating Scale: 1=Strongly Disagree 2=Disagree 3=Neutral 4=Agree 5=Strongly Agree					
My organizational culture is innovative, including all employees and relevant customers in the innovation process.					
I am innovative. I am intentional about innovation, engaging with customers and other employees at all levels and disciplines to learn and develop solutions that exceed customers' expectations (internally and externally).					
I promote innovation in the workplace among my staff, peers, superiors, customers, and all stakeholders, enabling everyone to collaborate and learn from each other to innovate solutions that exceed customers' expectations (internally and externally).					

Commit to Personal & Organizational Changes

Based on what you know and have read regarding innovation and your personal assessment above, what are you committing to improve for yourself, your staff, peers, superiors, stakeholders, or others?

Commitment	Commitment Date	Target Date
1.		
2.		
3.		

Transform Your Thoughts

"By idolizing those whom we honor, we do a disservice both to them and to ourselves… We fail to recognize that we could go and do likewise.
Charles V. Willie, Professor & Author[32]

"By definition, innovation is a charge into the unknown."
Author Unknown[33]

"If you look at history, innovation doesn't come just from giving people incentives; it comes from creating environments where their ideas can connect."
Steven Johnson, Author[34]

"For good ideas and true innovation, you need human interaction, conflict, argument, debate."
Margaret Heffernan, Entrepreneur, Chief Executive and Author[35]

"Fail early to succeed sooner."
David Kelley, Founder of IDEO[36]

Leaders ACT to THRIVE!

CHAPTER **12**

Vision with Strategic Execution that Thrives

"Where there is no vision, there is no hope."
GEORGE WASHINGTON CARVER, SCIENTIST[1]

WHO WOULD HAVE thought today, in the 21st century, consumers and businesses alike would enjoy technologies once only imaginable in the television series, *The Jetsons*, which first aired in 1962?[2] Yes, George, Jane, Judy and Elroy showed the world how technology could shape the future—smartwatches, smart shoes, robotics, 3D printers, and drones. While all the technologies have not been fully realized, and will continue to evolve, vision was birthed!

Organizations and individuals need a vision to thrive; otherwise, no one knows where they are going or why they do what they do. They waste time, reacting to life versus being proactive and making a difference that matters most to the organization—its employees, customers, stakeholders, and life in all areas. A vision gives employees something they can wrap their arms around and get excited about. As the world evolves, the vision may also need to be updated to stay relevant. Leaders can facilitate this effort with:

- Vision (Creation, Communication and Commitment)
- Strategic Leadership in Thought, Action and Influence
- Strategic Foresight for Future Expansion

Vision (Creation, Communication and Commitment)

Vision is a crucial ingredient to leadership success.[3] Regardless of leadership style, every leader must have a vision no matter the magnitude. It stimulates passion and enthusiasm in the leader and ultimately in the followers. For example, the late Steve Jobs was not considered a natural leader, but he had a vision about computers and software that transformed the way people work and communicate.

"A vision is not a dream but a reality that has yet to come into existence."[4] Vision provides focus.[5] It generates energy and emotion that excite others to embrace it and enter the race to realize it. It empowers the leader and the organization to continue the mission and cross the finish line.[6] When leaders birth true vision and employees feel the passion and commitment of the leader, they do not just follow the leader out of duty, they are inspired to follow the leader.[7]

When developing a vision, effective leaders know that the status quo does not work and they challenge it.[8] They think beyond the present to determine future possibilities for making a difference in the world. They manage the fears of failure that may hinder success.[9] They understand that failure is part of the learning process and they should expect it sometimes.

Leaders also invite the team to be a part of the vision development.[10] Employees can participate in the brainstorming sessions or have opportunities to submit ideas, understanding that leaders welcome all ideas regardless of how crazy or bad the employees may think their ideas are. One idea leads to another idea that is enhanced by another idea in the effort to create a shared vision that all can embrace and get excited about.

The creation of the vision goes hand-in-hand with the communication that appeals to the people and lays the foundation for commitment.[11] Therefore, once the leaders along with employees have developed the shared vision, which is simple, understandable and relatable, the leaders communicate the vision in such a way that people get it.[12] They can bring the vision to life and engage others with word pictures and storytelling.[13] The leader's genuineness, optimism, effective verbal and nonverbal communication, along with sharing emotions will spark others' interest, encouraging them to act or change.[14]

Besides sharing the big picture, leaders also communicate the details of how the vision will come to fruition and how it affects employees.[15] As the employees understand the vision, the question becomes—"Is the vision worthy of [their] commitment?"[16] With commitment, leaders and employees work together to make the necessary adjustments for alignment of personal and corporate visions and goals with full support. Together, they create a partnership in realizing the vision.

Strategic Leadership in Thought, Action and Influence

Strategic leadership is a continuous process of thinking, acting, and influencing the present and future posture of an organization, discipline, product line, or service.[17] It requires an understanding of the internal and external forces challenging growth and sustainability, and the ability to prioritize effectively, balancing short-term and long-term goals to achieve the vision. Strategic leadership includes lifelong learning to minimize the risk of stagnation and obsoleteness. It includes a learning environment wherein the team members think, act, and influence with a strategic mindset (Table 12.1).[18]

Table 12.1

Strategic Skills and Mindset	
Skills	**Mindset**
Strategic Thinking	• Strategic thinking is a collective process. • Strategic thinking is about the present, not just the future. • Strategic thinking has an artful side as well as a rigorous and analytical side.
Strategic Acting	• Only some actions are strategic. • Strategic acting is both short term and long term. • Strategic acting is an opportunity for learning. • Strategic decisions always involve uncertainty.
Strategic Influencing	• Strategic influence requires more than persuasion. • Strategic influence is far reaching. • It's as important to be open to influence as it is to influence others. • Strategic influence starts with a hard look at yourself.

Extracted from Hughes, Beatty, and Dinwoodie (2014), 55, 105, 148.

Strategic leaders ensure all managers at all levels, including individual contributors, exemplify this strategic behavior of thinking, acting, and influencing as leaders provide "direction, alignment, and commitment" to the organization,[19] focusing and allocating resources on the rights initiatives.[20]

As long-term planning and strategic foresight are vital to the health of the organization,[21] in a dynamic, global marketplace, organizations must practice continuous strategic planning.[22] To this end, developing a plan to sit on the shelf until the following year is no longer relevant. Leaders involve team members at all levels of the organization in the continuous strategic planning process, which builds an emotional, psychological commitment among employees as they explore and analyze ideas in a fun, relaxed environment.[23] This inclusion, along with the team's vision, inspires hope for the future by enabling the followers to see a significant difference in the current versus future states.[24] This approach to strategic planning is something everyone can get excited about and commit to achieving.

Strategic Thought

Being strategic is multifaceted as depicted in the strategic mindset framework. When leaders strive to become more strategic in their thinking, they consider the organizational vision, the competition, innovation, and creative thinking.[25] Primary activities for developing and enhancing strategic mindset include the SWOT analysis, examining the internal strengths and weaknesses, and the external opportunities and threats.[26] Including analysis tools like STEEPLE (social, technological, economic, environmental, political, legal, and ethical)[27] can enable a more comprehensive analysis, addressing the driving forces impacting the product or industry with strategic foresight into the future (i.e., 10 or more years ahead). Other variants of the analysis include STEEP (without the legal and ethical components)[28] or PESTLE,[29] a rearrangement of STEEPLE without ethics (i.e., political, economic, social, technological, legal, and environmental).

Interaction with customers is another means of thinking strategically.[30] It enables the organization to explore, understand and define the business problems and challenges to facilitate the creation of fresh ideas for the future. Employees live life with customers to get this detailed understanding of their challenges that lead to win-win-win solutions.

Strategic Action and Influence

Within an organization, there is always something vying for one's time (e.g., meetings, decisions, customer challenges, report writing) such that people conclude they are constantly "acting."[31] However, strategic acting is different; it is about building competitive differentiation with the commitment of resources.[32] While there is interdependence with strategic thinking, strategic acting is the actual execution—the commitment of resources, the appointment of project leaders, and taking thinking to the next level to yield the best return on investment.

To be effective, leaders and managers also have to have strategic influence, developing and maintaining relationships inside and outside the organization.[33] This influence has to be long term, based on trust, credibility, self-awareness, and authenticity, appealing to the heart (emotions) and not just the head. Leaders recognize and understand that because internal and external environments change, support for a decision today does not guarantee future support. Therefore, maintaining relationships is crucial for future success. Leaders have to be other-centered, understanding their values and concerns and have the self-awareness and openness to the possibilities of being influenced as well.

Strategic influence is also essential when supporting and promoting innovative behavior among team members.[34] Leaders should welcome creative ideas from employees even when refinement is needed as one thought can generate other ideas. Embracing innovation also requires leaders to exercise strategic influence to ward off antibodies or the naysayers (i.e., persons comfortable with the status quo) while balancing current and future innovation projects.

When leaders embrace and promote strategic leadership (i.e., strategic thinking, acting, and influencing) at all levels, everyone wins as they have access to customers and information that can contribute to the success of the organization.[35] Strategic leadership along with strategic foresight enables effectiveness and efficiency to allocate the right resources toward the right initiatives, crisis management, and risk mitigation.[36] It also helps control scope creep on projects as everyone is thinking strategically. The organization can also plan better for the future by assessing needs (e.g., skills and training) to equip the workforce. While being strategic can be time consuming, the organization, employees, customers, and stakeholders are all the better for it—they thrive.

Strategic Foresight for Future Expansion

Leaders can enhance strategic thinking with strategic foresight, ensuring the vision carries the organization into the future with continuous evolution as needed. Strategic foresight is defined as "the ability to anticipate and assess future events as well as to strategize to avert future dangers and grasp future opportunities."[37] Strategic foresight enables leaders and employees to develop successful, long-term strategies, mitigate risks with contingencies, and prepare for the future.

One challenge of strategic foresight is sometimes having limited or imperfect data that may require action. Leaders and employees alike have to get comfortable with the fact that some information may not be accurate or precise, which can still guide one's preparation for the future or save lives. General Colin Powell once said, "If you can tell me with a hundred percent certainty that we are going to be bombed, it is too late for me to do anything about it."[38] Likewise, foresight can enable organizations to improve the future but not predict it.[39] Provided in Table 12.2 is a strategic foresight framework based on the best practices from futurists in academia and the consulting industry.[40]

These phases do not have to be executed in this exact order, although most futurist follow this sequence of steps. Nevertheless, these collective activities and associated strategic tools will help an organization shape its future, being prepared with innovative solutions to solve tomorrow's problems.

Table 12.2

Strategic Foresight Framework	
Phases	**Description**
Framing Organization of the Issues	Scoping the Problems: attitude, audience, work environment, rationale and purpose, objectives, and teams.
Scanning Organizational Context	Gathering Information: the system, history and context of the issue, and how to scan for information regarding the future of the issue.
Forecasting "What Will Be" May Not Be	Identifying Baseline and Alternative Futures: drivers and uncertainties, tools, diverging and converging approaches, and alternatives.
Visioning From Potentiality to the Desired Future	Determining a Preferred Future: implications of the forecast, and envisioning designed outcomes.
Planning Building the Bridge Between Vision & Strategy	Planning to Realize the Vision: strategy and options for carrying out the vision.
Acting Execution	Executing the Plan: communicating the results, developing action agendas, and institutionalizing strategic thinking and intelligence systems.

Adapted from Hines (2006), 19-21.

Conclusion

Without vision, there is no purpose or fuel to move the organization forward. Without a strategy, there is no "how." Organizations need both to succeed—to thrive. The more leaders include employees at all levels in the vision development and strategic planning process, connecting with the heart and emotions, the higher the passion and commitment to the execution and realization of the vision. As the world continuously evolves, leaders and employees at all levels have to stay in tune with internal and external environments to monitor and revise the vision and strategy continually for relevance. Leaders also have to ensure everyone is engaged in a continuous learning process and are empowered to realize the vision. Their commitment from the head and the heart will enable the win-win-win for all to thrive!

Chapter 12 - The Vision ACT

Assess Your Attitude & Actions

Based on the content of this chapter, please assess your leadership and influence in establishing vision with strategic execution within the organizational culture.

Chapter 12 Assessment	1	2	3	4	5
Rating Scale: 1=Strongly Disagree 2=Disagree 3=Neutral 4=Agree 5=Strongly Agree					
My organizational culture includes everyone in the vision and strategy development and execution. My organization continuously promotes and practices strategic thinking, acting, influencing, and futuring.					
I have a clear vision and continuously practice strategic thinking, acting, influencing, and futuring. I am inclusive in the development of corporate vision and strategy.					
I promote inclusion in the vision and strategy development, and execution among my staff, peers, superiors, and all stakeholders, enabling and supporting their strategic thinking, acting, influencing and futuring.					

Commit to Personal & Organizational Changes

Based on what you know and have read regarding vision with strategic execution, what are you committing to improve for yourself, your staff, peers, superiors, stakeholders, or others?

Commitment	Commitment Date	Target Date
1.		
2.		
3.		

Transform Your Thoughts

*"A leader has the vision and conviction that a dream can be achieved.
He inspires the power and energy to get it done."*
Ralph Lauren, Fashion Designer[41]

*"Good leaders have vision and inspire others to help them turn vision into reality.
Great leaders create more leaders, not followers.
Great leaders have vision, share vision, and inspire others to create their own."*
Roy T. Bennett, Author, *The Light in the Heart*[42]

"The first step toward creating an improved future is developing the ability to envision it. VISION will ignite the fire of passion that fuels our commitment to do WHATEVER IT TAKES to achieve excellence. Only VISION allows us to transform dreams of greatness into the reality of achievement through human action. VISION has no boundaries and knows no limits. Our VISION is what we become in life."
Tony Dungy, Football Coach & Author[43]

Leaders ACT to THRIVE!

CHAPTER **13**

Empowerment to Thrive

*"Empowerment isn't a buzzword among leadership gurus.
It's a proven technique where leaders give their teams the
appropriate training, tools, resources, and guidance to succeed."*
JOHN RAMPTON, BUSINESSMAN & AUTHOR[1]

WHILE VISION, INTEGRITY, and commitment to employees, customers, and shareholders have been keys to leadership success in the past and will continue in the future, tomorrow's leaders will also need to share and distribute leadership.[2] Leaders will need to empower their employees, which is one of the best gifts leaders give their team. So what is empowerment? What does it look like? Empowerment is the "power sharing, the delegation of power or authority to subordinates in the organization… It addresses three higher-level needs that truly motivate people—the desire for mastery, a sense of autonomy, and the need for a driving purpose…"[3] It is a motivational element to help employees with self-efficacy, knowing they are making a difference. Empowerment enables employees to bring their complete self to work and not "leave their brains at the door" while enabling organizations to embrace, develop and reward employees for their "intellectual capital."[4]

In ancient history, Moses' life as the leader and judge of the Israelites provides an excellent example of leadership without delegation and the value of empowerment.[5] Once Moses led the Israelites out of Egypt, where they were enslaved, he had a major responsibility of handling their issues and judging the people. Jethro, Moses' father-in-law, observed Moses' activities and process, and out of care and concern for Moses and the people, Jethro advised Moses that his method for judging the people's matters was not working for him nor the people; they all became exhausted. Jethro then provided a strategy and execution plan for organizing and judging the people. He also shared the selection criteria for choosing leaders (e.g., competent, honest men of integrity). He recommended that Moses divine the people in groups of tens, fifties, hundreds, and thousands with leaders at every level—a hierarchy of delegated responsibilities. The leaders handled the minor cases at their levels while sending the major cases to Moses. This action created a peaceful and manageable win-win-win solution.

This story highlights how leaders, like Moses, can run themselves ragged in trying to be everything to everybody where nobody wins, especially when there are team members available, willing, and able to share the load of taking on more leadership responsibilities and being involved in the decision-making process. It also demonstrates the benefits of relinquishing some responsibilities and empowering employees to lead.[6] Empowerment enables employees to be more productive and customer-focused, yielding higher quality work. They contribute more ideas and initiatives, creating a better innovative organization. Employees also enjoy a democratic environment with flexibility versus the hierarchical, stringent structure with controlling managers. There are higher levels of commitment and job satisfaction, less work-related stress, and lower attrition. Leaders enable empowerment through:

- Vision and Strategy
- Organizational Structure and Job Design
- Data and Information
- Systems, Tools and Processes
- Resources
- Timely Decisions
- Removal of Roadblocks
- Freedom to Act
- Confidence and Encouragement

Vision and Strategy

Although vision and strategy creation was addressed in the previous chapter and other sections of this book, the emphasis of this chapter is to give employees the total picture to facilitate empowerment. They need more than just tasks and projects assigned or delegated to them. They need to understand the "what" and the "why." When employees know and are involved in creating the vision and strategy, they are empowered to give more than what is requested or expected as they see the end goal or desired state and can add their creative juices to exceed expectations. From a psychological perspective, employees must have the knowledge, information, project significance, discretion, and rewards for complete empowerment.[7] They will enjoy a sense of ownership as their personal mission is aligned with their organization's mission.[8]

Hilcorp Energy, a producer of onshore natural gas and crude oil, based in Houston, Texas, attributed the success of the company to their associates (i.e., people on the frontline) who were engaged and empowered. Leaders gave these managers decision-making authority and were transparent with the financial and operations information to enable them to make thoughtful, informed decisions. They earned bonuses up to 60 percent of their yearly salaries based on corporate performance, and they also had the option to invest in other Hilcorp projects.

Organizational Structure and Job Design

The organizational structure and job design can hinder or facilitate empowerment. When leaders design and structure the organization appropriately, aligning it with the strategic direction, employees can play well together with all the pieces fitting together like a beautiful puzzle. Without an appropriately designed structure, employees may encounter roadblocks, deal with people with different priorities and timelines, or lose time figuring out ways to get things done—all contributing to frustration and lost productivity with associated costs. The solution includes an organizational design and structure that take into consideration the organizational goals and strategies, along with an understanding of the basic tasks, decision makers, and communication structure.[9] The structure needs to facilitate employees' support, access to resources and information, and opportunities to learn and grow.[10]

Along with the organizational structure, leaders can facilitate empowerment with the job design so that employees experience more autonomy, purpose, and empowerment.[11] Five essential elements of the job design to enable empowerment include:

1. Skill Diversity: The job design should include a variety of skills to enhance the employee's motivation.
2. Start-Finish Project: The employee should be engaged from the beginning to the end with total ownership and defined completion criteria.
3. Value Creation: Employees need to know their job is essential, adding value to customers or the organization.
4. Autonomy: The employee is excited about their assignment when they have the flexibility to plan and execute without micromanagement.
5. Feedback and Results: Leaders should provide constructive feedback to employees and help them know how their work is contributing to the organization in fulfilling the mission. Employees especially need this input when results are not as tangible (e.g., research, conference speakers).

These elements of the job design facilitate the transition of leaders' responsibilities to employees while creating job satisfaction, performance, growth, and learning opportunities.

Data and Information

Leaders also have to empower people with the information they need to succeed. As there is much data and information at people's disposal, this access contributes to information overload. And, yet people still need information that may not be tracked or readily available, or it may come with a hefty price tag (e.g., industry analysts' reports). Therefore, leaders have to ensure the right data is captured and accessible within the organization, implementing the systems, tools and processes to facilitate this effort. They also need to provide employees with external information—industry and market reports to do their jobs. Otherwise, employees may struggle to get meaningful data or lose productivity piecing information together. Sometimes the challenge may be acceptable, considering the cost-benefit.

Systems, Tools and Processes

Employees need access to systems, tools and processes to be productive and empowered. And, as technology is disrupting everything, changing the way people work, access information, and communicate, it has a snowball effect on other technologies people want or need to be effective personally and professionally.[12] For example, mobile devices create the need for work-related mobile applications for employees to access information and perform their jobs from any location or device at any time. Therefore, systems have to enable information sharing, communication, collaboration, and coordination among various departments,[13] leveraging relevant technologies and devices.

Processes provide a framework for accomplishing goals and completing tasks for consistent performance throughout the department.[14] They "define the patterns of interaction, coordination, communication, and decision making that people use to get work done. Processes are agreements or political alliances between management and staff in which resources are promised to [enable the completion of] work in a certain way."[15] Processes enable long-term success and sustainability while providing an opportunity for learning and sharing best practices; they are documented and continuously improved for efficiency.

Leaders have a crucial role in ensuring these systems, tools, and processes are working correctly based on input and feedback from their teams. Where possible, tools, and processes have to be simplified or automated. When there are challenges, leaders can use their position, authority, and influence to resolve them. Sometimes leaders and managers consume their time being involved in activities that lower-level employees can do. Teams will be more effective with leaders addressing the interdepartmental, cultural or corporate problems so that employees can focus on the team's deliverables.

Leaders also empower employees by staying abreast of the latest technology and associated effects on the organization to improve processes, decision making, and learning. In addition, they ensure a healthy, balanced usage of tools and technology and not use technology for technology's sake. If it is not adding value to the process, why use it?

Resources

Besides the resources described above, empowerment also requires a strategic allocation of financial and human resources to fulfill their responsibilities. When leaders do not address this critical element, they set employees up for failure. Yes, there may be a need for employees' creativity to achieve the goal; however, leaders must be realistic about the resources and adjust expectations accordingly. Otherwise, they are not leading; they are delegating at the expense of employees and the organization. When there are too few resources, everyone needs to determine strategically what the team will and will not do. There can also be times, when there are too many people involved, requiring reallocation or removal of resources. Otherwise, when there are too many cooks in the kitchen, people step all over each other, affecting productivity and efficient usage of resources.

Timely Decisions

According to Ralph Waldo Emerson, "the speed of the leader determines the rate of the pack;"[16] therefore, leaders empower teams with their timely actions, including decision making. When there are deadlines and deliverables quickly approaching, employees do not want leadership decisions or actions to hinder progress. Similar to resource management, leaders can minimize the time for decision making by focusing on leadership responsibilities while delegating tasks and some decision-making activities to other staff members at the various levels, equipping them with the pertinent information to make informed decisions.

Leaders can equip employees for effective decision making by exposing them to opportunities wherein employees can learn how their boss and other leaders think and make decisions. For example, leaders can include them in strategic meetings and other decision-making activities (e.g., project approval meetings, etc.). The empowered staff members can then think through the discussions and decisions made during these strategic meetings and apply this knowledge when needing to act on their boss' behalf, discerning when to engage their leaders in more significant challenges. In essence, the delegation of responsibilities and some decision making frees time for the leader to lead more effectively and efficiently and make timely decisions.

Removal of Roadblocks

Roadblocks can manifest themselves in the form of relentless personnel who refuse to change or help with the resolution,[17] outdated policies, procedures, programs, systems, tools, and technologies. These challenges may also include interdepartmental conflict, misaligned project priorities, resource limitations or escalations when employees' efforts are unsuccessful. In addition, the team culture may be difficult and uncomfortable, and there may be other obstacles requiring the leader to assess the situation and make the necessary changes. Doing nothing is not leadership. When necessary, leaders have to leverage their position, power, and authority to influence the required change.

Freedom to Act

When leaders empower their teams, they give them the freedom to act without micromanagement. Leaders equip employees with the tools—the knowledge, vision, strategy, and guidelines—to act on the leader's behalf in meetings internally and externally. This detail helps the employees know what they are doing and why so that when unanticipated topics are addressed or issues arise, the empowered employee can engage in meaningful dialogue and be confident and comfortable making decisions as needed, including the ability to alter structure, systems, and procedures that the leaders may have created[18] within reason as long as the change does not negatively affect other groups. To this end, leaders and employees have to have mutual understanding and meaningful communications channels (e.g., progress reports, team meetings, and one-to-one meetings) for overall team effectiveness and vision realization.

Confidence and Encouragement

Leaders promote empowerment by encouraging their employees and expressing their confidence (i.e., belief and trust) in them through words and actions. Leaders delegate responsibilities they know their followers can succeed and grow in.[19] This delegation of responsibilities inspires and encourages the employees with the confidence they need to accomplish the assignment while creating a positive, enthusiastic work environment wherein people can enjoy their work as they grow.

Leaders empower through affirmation. They communicate the "Yes, you can" encouragement. They share positive and constructive feedback. When weaknesses are identified or expressed, leaders coach their employees regarding a plan to overcome the challenges. If the employee does not need the skill for the current job or future career goals, leaders can coach them to channel their energy to other goals, strategically managing time and resources.

Conclusion

Leaders understand and empower their teams by adopting a servant leader's mindset. Ken Blanchard, management expert and author, says it is "all about making the goals clear and then rolling your sleeves up and doing whatever it takes to help people win. In this situation, [employees] don't work for you, you work for them."[20] Leaders proactively and strategically supply their team members with the resources they need to succeed, including creating a healthy, collaborative work culture, and resolving any associated roadblocks. Leaders are fair in decision making, distribution of projects, and recognition.[21] They create a win-win-win and thrive!

As there are challenges with empowerment, leaders provide the managers and employees with the vision and support they need for the journey.[22] Some employees may not understand the value of empowerment and the impact it will have on them while others may not want the accountability for work they are not controlling; and therefore, may feel threatened and fearful of losing their jobs. Leaders can mitigate this concern through communication, training, and clear expectations.

Leaders should also harmonize the empowerment of employees with support of the organization's vision and values. They discern when to release power, whom to empower, and when to lend a helping hand for overall success. They allow mistakes to be a part of the learning experience to enable future success.

Chapter 13 - The Empowerment ACT

Assess Your Attitude & Actions

Based on the content of this chapter, please assess your leadership and influence in empowering others to thrive.

Chapter 13 Assessment	1	2	3	4	5
Rating Scale: 1=Strongly Disagree 2=Disagree 3=Neutral 4=Agree 5=Strongly Agree					
My organizational culture enables empowerment for employees at all levels.					
I am empowered and equipped with the information and tools I need to thrive in my role.					
I promote empowerment in the workplace among my staff, peers, superiors, and all stakeholders, sharing and equipping everyone with the information and tools they need to thrive.					

Commit to Personal & Organizational Changes

Based on what you know and have read regarding empowerment and your personal assessment above, what are you committing to improve for yourself, your staff, peers, superiors, stakeholders, or others?

Commitment	Commitment Date	Target Date
1.		
2.		
3.		

Transform Your Thoughts

*"As we look ahead into the next century,
leaders will be those who empower others."*
Bill Gates, Founder of the Microsoft Corporation & American Businessman[23]

*"My idea of management is that what your job is as the boss
is to find really good people and empower them and leave them alone."*
Ruth Reichl, Chef & Author[24]

*"In the past, a leader was a boss. Today's leaders must be partners with their
people...they no longer can lead solely based on positional power."*
Ken Blanchard, Management Expert & Author[25]

Leaders ACT to THRIVE!

CHAPTER **14**

Now THRIVE²!

> *"Leaders need to embrace and master the art of transformation for their organizations to thrive."*
> STEVEN J. BOWEN, AUTHOR[1]

THRIVE! WHO WOULD not be excited to work for a thriving organization as envisioned in this book? Leaders can lead and employees can follow in an organization filled with trust, respect, and ethical and fair practices where everyone is committed to excellence and can use their holistic self (e.g., skills, knowledge, experience and interest) as they work together to realize the corporate vision and associated goals. People will stand in line to walk through the doors of a healthy organization with a positive image among employees, customers, and external community as they exceed customers and shareholders' expectations. Who does not want to thrive for the win-win-win, a win for the organization, a win for employees, and a win for customers and communities?

While everyone may be excited, leaders may also feel overwhelmed, thinking this THRIVE² culture is only a dream and impossible to achieve with no time to affect the appropriate changes. Quite the opposite! This thriving culture is attainable and maintainable with commitment, passion, hard work and courageous leadership. Although all persons in the organization impact the culture and its success, leaders have the arduous and rewarding task of setting the vision and affecting positive change. Therefore, they can empower their teams to run the business so they can enable a thriving organizational culture as they plan and promote:

- Sincerity and Intentionality in Living and Leading the Culture
- Plans and Communication for Change
- Assessment and Development of the Right Team

- Courageous HR Leadership and Support
- Understanding and Alignment of the Organizational Culture Components
- Continuous Training
- Courageous Leadership
- Responsibility and Ownership - A Word to CEOs and Board Members
- Fun and Celebration

Sincerity and Intentionality in Living and Leading the Culture

Creating a thriving culture will not just happen.[2] Leaders along with HR professionals must develop and nurture the THRIVE² culture, being sincere and intentional in their attitudes and actions. They cannot pretend to be what they are not. They genuinely have to be the culture and make changes where needed. They have to ACT (assess, commit, and transform) — assess attitude and actions, commit to personal and organizational changes, and transform their thoughts.

If leaders are sincere about the success of the organization, they have to be honest with themselves regarding their willingness and ability to live, lead, and promote the desired culture. If their personal assessment determines a misalignment with the desired culture, they have to assess if they want to change or do they want to move on. If they wish to be a part of the organization and promote the desired culture, they have to be intentional in their ACT to transform themselves and the organization to be the culture, living and leading others down the thriving road. With commitment and action, they can and will be the example and hold others accountable for cultivating this win-win-win culture.

In essence, leaders personify the culture they want, which means they are living it in every area of life. The employees, customers, and community see the culture in them as they are the same person in and out of the office—no pretense. As they live the culture, they lead the culture with their actions speaking louder than their words.

Plans and Communication for Change

Leaders have to be intentional as they develop a vision and associated communication and strategic plans for the desired culture change, helping employees understand the existing culture, the desired culture and the required changes.[3] They need to communicate the importance of the change, how the change will improve the organization over time,[4] the elements of the change, and associated goals and milestones.[5]

The communication and strategic plans are made and executed with the understanding that everyone will not embrace the cultural change and may even resist it.[6] This resistance can be mitigated or thwarted as leaders help employees to not only understand the purpose of the change, but also provide opportunities for them to address their feelings and concerns. When leaders engage in this exchange of information, they demonstrate their care and value for the employees, which is critical to success.

The plans will also include updating processes to support the desired change (e.g., learning, innovation, and ethics). Rewards and disciplines will be a part of the plan to encourage the desired behavior.[7] Leader may also select champions at various levels to help promote the culture change.[8]

Assessment and Development of the Right Team

Assuming that leaders have gone through their personal assessment and are aligned with the preferred culture, they have to assess and build their teams with the personnel (i.e., leaders, employees, and potential future leaders) who have the desired character and competence.[9] Having the right skills and experiences is excellent and has become a deciding factor in hiring and retaining personnel. However, the employees and candidates must fit in with the preferred culture, having the core values, heart, and right attitude to embrace it. If they have the character and competence, they can learn anything they need to know to fulfill their functional responsibilities.

As there may be some leaders transitioning to the culture or may not have totally embraced it, there has to be a check and balance to minimize the risk of these leaders recruiting and hiring the wrong people. Organizations can minimize this possibility by including a list of required character and culture related interview questions to ask and document responses during the interview. In additional, having at least one interviewer (e.g., HR personnel) on the hiring team to serve as the culture assessor (i.e., a neutral party and culture promoter) can help with this evaluation.

When hiring and developing leaders to lead and promote the desired organizational culture, the ideal is having leaders with transformational leadership qualities with whom followers can relate.[10] They have the charisma, "the power to influence, gain trust, excite and motivate followers." These leaders are mindful of their followers' needs and focus on meeting them. They and their employees are engaged in reaching extraordinary goals, and in the process, employees transform to leaders, maturing in their leadership as their leaders become models or moral agents.

Courageous HR Leadership and Support

HR professionals have a significant role to play as they can help create, deliver, and transform the desired culture.[11] They are a critical factor in ensuring the success of the culture transformation and maintenance as they have the ability and functional position to hold leaders and employees accountable to the cultural practices and establish the rewards and disciplinary actions to promote the desired culture. If leaders and employees are to take the cultural mandates seriously, HR has to be reliable in fulfilling their functional role and ensuring everyone does the same. They cannot allow a leader's power, position and influence prevent them from doing the right thing in facilitating a healthy, thriving culture. Therefore, such factors as courageous leadership, conflict management, risk taking, and personal sacrifice become part of the hiring criteria for HR personnel with accountability to senior leadership and board members.

Understanding and Alignment of the Organizational Culture Components

There are several components that make up the organizational culture—explicit behaviors, artifacts, conscious contracts and norms, and implicit assumptions (Exhibit 14.1 and Table 14.1).[12] Leaders have to ensure alignment of these components with no conflicting messaging to employees or customers. For example, if the vision and mission statements reflect the significance of customers and customer service, performance metrics will not allow a customer to be on hold with customer service for a long time. Leaders cannot have signs on the walls that talk about respecting people and then employees hear an executive yell and curse at his secretary. Every culture element must align.

Exhibit 14. 1

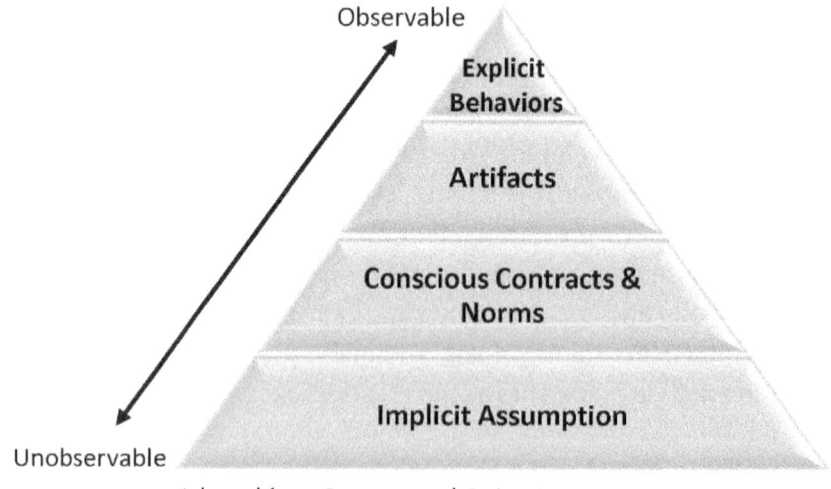

Adapted from Cameron and Quinn (2011), 19–20.

Table 14.1

Organizational Culture Components	
Components	**Explanation or Examples**
Explicit Behaviors (Most Obvious Expression of the Culture)	The way employees interact: • How much they are allowed to be themselves, how much they are motivated to be creative. • "Just the way things are done around here."
Artifacts	Cultural elements that are more noticeable: • Office buildings, furniture, office space, work attire. • Vision and mission statements, logos, themes. • Goals and recognition.
Conscious Contracts & Norms	Guidelines, policies, and procedures that inform employees of how to work with each other to achieve mutual goals or what one needs to do to be rewarded or promoted.
Implicit Assumptions (Most Fundamental Level)	The human factors relative to the environment that only become known when they conflict with other competing or contradictory factors (e.g., primary language).

Adapted from Cameron and Quinn (2011), 19–20.

Continuous Training

Besides the communication and strategic plans for cultural change, continuous training is critical to the success of the cultural change journey. All employees must take part in culture training (in-person); this training is also a key element of the new hire training program. The culture development and maintenance process should also include required refresher training in various methods or formats (e.g., in-person, video-based) along with coaching and mentoring sessions and appraisal assessments to ensure transformation.

Courageous Leadership

Leaders have to be courageous in affecting cultural change and doing the right thing despite the challenges. They must be bold in living and leading the culture and holding everyone accountable to talking and walking the culture. Regardless of title, responsibility, or position, leaders have to encourage team members (e.g., followers, peers and superiors) to be courageous in promoting and protecting the culture, including addressing misdeeds or seeking support when needed regardless of one's title or position.

Responsibility and Ownership - A Word to CEOs and Board Members

While leaders at every level are responsible for the culture, the primary responsibility of the culture sits on the shoulders of the CEO and board members. CEOs and board members own the culture as some employees (even senior leaders) may not embrace the preferred culture, creating gaps in attitudes and actions among the leaders and managers on the organizational chart between the CEO and individual contributors. Also, HR may not support the culture as reflected in how they manage conflict when one party is not living the culture, possibly allowing leaders' positions and titles to influence the outcome of conflict resolution at the detriment of the employees and organization as a whole. Essentially, board members, CEOs and senior leadership who are far removed from the day-to-day operations have to take the time to observe, assess and determine the appropriate actions to ensure a thriving culture as anyone not living the culture can derail the culture. CEOs and board members have to hold all senior leaders accountable to ACT in order to transform and maintain the preferred culture. Likewise, the senior leaders also have to hold other leaders, managers and employees accountable to living the culture.

Fun and Celebration

As everyone spends so much time at work, why not enjoy it? If people enjoy it, it is not work! In a thriving culture, leaders and employees partner together to create and support an environment wherein everyone looks forward to work. Everyone enjoys their functional role while intentionally ensuring their fellow teammates have a wonderful day—being kind, respectful, and helpful, and having a grand time with a laugh or two. Even when there is conflict, which leaders, managers, and employees should expect sometimes, the relative parties will address it privately, in a caring, tactful, and respectful way, keeping the employees whole and loving life.

The team also takes time to have fun inside and outside the office environment, appealing to the various interests of the group. They proactively celebrate and recognize birthdays, personal successes, and team victories. These celebrations can help create a genuinely enjoyable work environment where everyone can thrive, looking forward to work every day—not dreading Mondays.

Conclusion

Like Howard Schultz, the late Samuel Truett Cathy (Founder of Chick-fil-A), the late Mary Kay Ash (Founder of Mary Kay Inc.), and other renown CEOs built businesses based on their values and succeeded as leaders in their industry. They demonstrated the importance of a thriving culture of treating people right, resulting in a formidable brand, exceptional performance, and satisfied customers and employees.

They showed that culture, which defines the way people work together based on their shared beliefs, values, and assumptions,[13] is the critical ingredient for an organization's success as it lays the foundation for the rewarding realization of organizational goals and desired changes.[14] A winning culture enabled companies like Walmart to compete successfully against Sears and Kmart, and Apple against Microsoft. Culture is the essential element that will allow organizations to thrive. It is and will be a critical factor in winning or losing with a multi-generational workforce wherein millennials have become the most dominant generation (e.g., within the US workforce, millennials are projected to make up at least 75% by 2025).[15]

Leaders throughout the world need to ensure their organizational culture provides what this blended workforce not only wants but needs. They have to ensure the work environment facilitates globalization, digitalization, innovation, social responsibility and all other transformations required to be a powerful player in the marketplace, making a difference for the betterment of others.

Besides performing well and reaping the results that keep board members and shareholders happy, the most significant reward for the leader is living and leading a leadership legacy that others (i.e., their business colleagues and family members) will want to not only follow but to emulate. The organization wins. The employees win. The customers and communities win. The families win. When leaders ACT, they live, lead and influence a culture that thrives and everyone wins. Leaders act to thrive and thrive to win.

Chapter 14 - The THRIVE² ACT

Assess Your Attitude & Actions

Based on the content of this chapter, please assess your leadership responsibility and influence in helping the organization THRIVE.²

Chapter 14 Assessment	1	2	3	4	5
Rating Scale: 1=Strongly Disagree 2=Disagree 3=Neutral 4=Agree 5=Strongly Agree					
My organization's leaders (i.e., CEO, board members, leaders and HR staff) partner together to promote and enable a thriving, win-win-win culture.					
I courageously live and lead a thriving, win-win-win culture, focusing on the job of leadership and leaving a legacy of leadership for others to follow.					
I partner with my staff, peers, superiors, HR personnel, and all stakeholders in living and leading a thriving, win-win-win culture, holding each other accountable to developing and maintaining a thriving culture wherein everyone wins.					

Commit to Personal & Organizational Changes

Based on what you know and have read regarding the significance of a healthy, thriving culture and your personal assessment above, what are you committing to improve for yourself, your staff, peers, superiors, stakeholders, or others?

Commitment	Commitment Date	Target Date
1.		
2.		
3.		

Transform Your Thoughts

"Change will not come if we wait for some other person or some other time. We are the ones we've been waiting for. We are the change that we seek."
President Barack Obama[16]

"If human beings are perceived as potentials rather than problems, as possessing strengths instead of weaknesses, as unlimited rather than dull and unresponsive, then they thrive and grow to their capabilities."
Barbara Bush, First Lady[17]

"By union the smallest states thrive. By discord the greatest are destroyed."
Sallust, Historian[18]

"If you don't put anything in place, do not expect miraculous results to appear."
Germany Kent, Journalist & Author[19]

"Inspiration may come from many places but motivation—the love of life, daily drive and the will to thrive—that must come from you from within."
Rasheed Ogunlaru, Life Coach, Speaker & Author[20]

"My mission in life is not merely to survive, but to thrive; and to do so with some passion, some compassion, some humor, and some style."
Maya Angelou, Poet[21]

Leaders ACT to THRIVE!

THRIVE²

CHARACTER	COMPETENCE
Trust	Teamwork
Health	Holism
Respect	Responsibility
Image	Innovation
Values	Vision
Ethics	Empowerment

Downloadable from www.leadershippassport.com/bookresources

Endnotes

Book Beginning

1. "Edgar Schein Quotes," AZquotes, accessed March 15, 2020, https://www.azquotes.com/quote/935762.

Chapter 1

1. "Adam Grant Quotes," Brainy Quote, accessed February 4, 2020, https://www.brainyquote.com/quotes/adam_grant_834202.

2. Howard Schultz, *Pour Your Heart Into It* (New York: Hyperion, 1997), 5.

3. Schultz, *Pour Your Heart Into It*, 4.

4. Schultz, *Pour Your Heart Into It*, 5.

5. Schultz, *Pour Your Heart Into It*, 8.

6. Gary Oster, *The Light Prize: Perspectives on Christian Innovation* (Virginia Beach, VA: Positive Signs Media, 2011), 79.

7. Eric Ries, *The Lean Startup: How Today's Entrepreneurs Use Continuous Innovation to Create Radically Successful Businesses* (New York: Crown Business, 2011), 28.

8. Karl Vesper, *New Venture Mechanics* (New York: Prentice Hall College Division, 1993), 270.

9. Schultz, *Pour Your Heart Into It*, 5–7.

10. Jay Richards, *Money, Greed, and God* (New York: HarperOne, 2010), 7–8.

11. Schultz, *Pour Your Heart Into It*, 318–24.

12. Schultz, *Pour Your Heart Into It*, 7.

13. Schultz, *Pour Your Heart Into It*, 5.

14. Schultz, *Pour Your Heart Into It*, 6.

15. Edgar Schein, *Organizational Culture and Leadership* (San Francisco: Wiley, 2010), 18.

16. Mike Losey, Sue Meisinger, and Dave Ulrich, *The Future of Human Resource Management: 64 Thought Leaders Explore the Critical HR Issues of Today and Tomorrow* (Hoboken, NJ: Wiley, 2005), 156.

17. Kim Cameron and Robert Quinn, *Diagnosing and Changing Organizational Culture: Based On the Competing Values Framework* (San Francisco: Jossey-Bass, 2011), 22.

18. Marcella Bremer, *Organizational Culture Change: Unleashing Your Organization's Potential in Circles of 10* (Zwolle, Netherlands: Kikker Groep, 2012), 31.

19. Cameron and Quinn, *Diagnosing and Changing Organizational Culture,* 25.

20. Losey, Meisinger, and Ulrich, *The Future of Human Resource Management,* 153.

21. Losey, Meisinger, and Ulrich, *The Future of Human Resource Management,* 153.

22. Eric Flamholtz and Yvonne Randle, *Corporate Culture: The Ultimate Strategic Asset* (Redwood City, CA: Stanford University Press, 2011), 13.

23. Flamholtz and Randle, *Corporate Culture,* 14.

24. Flamholtz and Randle, *Corporate Culture,* 15.

25. Flamholtz and Randle, *Corporate Culture,* 17.

26. Flamholtz and Randle, *Corporate Culture,* 17–21.

27. Flamholtz and Randle, *Corporate Culture,* 20.

28. Flamholtz and Randle, *Corporate Culture,* 20–21.

29. Ken Hultman and Bill Gellermann, *Balancing Individual and Organizational Values: Walking the Tightrope to Success* (San Francisco: Jossey-Bass/Pfeiffer, 2002), 10–11.

30. Flamholtz and Randle, *Corporate Culture,* 17–21.

31. Flamholtz and Randle, *Corporate Culture,* 17–21.

32. Hultman and Gellermann, *Balancing Individual and Organizational Values,* 10–11.

33. Flamholtz and Randle, *Corporate Culture,* 18.

34. Deborah Hopen, "Editor's Notebook: Does Culture Eat Strategy?" *The Journal for Quality and Participation* 31, no. 2 (Summer 2008): 3.

35. "Adam Grant Quotes," BrainyQuote, accessed February 4, 2020, https://www.brainyquote.com/quotes/adam_grant_834203.

36. Peter Schroeder, "The 50 Most Inspirational Company Culture Quotes of All-Time," *Northpass,* accessed February 4, 2020, https://www.northpass.com/blog/the-50-most-inspirational-company-culture-quotes-of-all-time.

Chapter 2

1. "Warren Bennis Quotes," BrainyQuote, accessed February 4, 2020, https://www.brainyquote.com/quotes/warren_bennis_384360.

2. James Kouzes and Barry Posner, *The Leadership Challenge* (San Francisco: Jossey-Bass, 2012), 220.

3. *The Oxford Dictionary of Philosophy,* 3rd ed. (2016), s.v. "Trust."

4. David Maister, Charles Green, and Robert Galford, *The Trusted Advisor* (New York: Simon & Schuster, 2001), 7–16.

5. Ira Chaleff, *The Courageous Follower: Standing Up to and for Our Leaders* (San

Francisco: Berrett-Koehler, 2009), 29.

6. Gus Gordon and Jerry Gilley, "A Trust-Leadership Model," *Performance Improvement* 51, no. 7 (August 2012): 28.

7. Ian Sutherland, "Learning and Growing: Trust, Leadership, and Response to Crisis," *Journal of Educational Administration* 55, no. 1 (2017): 2.

8. Richard Daft, The Leadership Experience, 6th ed. (Stamford, CT: Cengage Learning, 2015), 298.

9. Kouzes and Posner, *The Leadership Challenge*, 220.

10. Gordon and Gilley, "A Trust-Leadership Model," 30.

11. Jo-Ann Byrne, "A Culture of Trust: Staff Development's Role in Enhancing Organizational Culture," *Strategies for Nurse Managers* (July 2010): 10–11.

12. Bruce Winston and Kathleen Patterson, "An Integrative Definition of Leadership," *International Journal of Leadership Studies* 1, no. 2 (2006): 6–32.

13. Stefan Klaussner, "Trust and Leadership: Toward an Interactive Perspective," *Journal of Change Management* 12, no. 4 (December 2012): 417.

14. Chaleff, *The Courageous Follower*, 29.

15. Bernard Bass and Ruth Bass, *The Bass Handbook of Leadership: Theory, Research, and Managerial Applications, 4th. ed.* (New York: Free Press, 2008), 258.

16. Nick Davis, "Executive Coaching Survey Shows Serious Lack of Trust in Leaders," *Davis Associates,* https://davisassociates.co.uk/executive-coaching-builds-trust/?utm_source=enoutreach&utm_medium=article.

17. Daft, *The Leadership Experience*, 40.

18. Bass and Bass, *The Bass Handbook of Leadership*, 258.

19. Gordon and Gilley, "A Trust-Leadership Model," 28.

20. Daft, *The Leadership Experience*, 40.

21. Gordon and Gilley, "A Trust-Leadership Model," 29.

22. Chaleff, *The Courageous Follower*, 29.

23. Klaussner, "Trust and Leadership," 427.

24. Chaleff, *The Courageous Follower*, 29.

25. Daft, *The Leadership Experience*, 40.

26. Kouzes and Posner, *The Leadership Challenge*, 226.

27. Robert Lussier, and Christopher Achua. *Leadership: Theory, Application, & Skill Development*, 5th ed. (Mason, OH: Cengage Learning, 2013), 336.

28. Gordon and Gilley, "A Trust-Leadership Model," 30.

29. Chaleff, *The Courageous Follower*, 29.

30. Daft, *The Leadership Experience*, 40.

31. Gordon and Gilley, "A Trust-Leadership Model," 30.

32. Chaleff, *The Courageous Follower*, 29.

33. Kouzes and Posner, *The Leadership Challenge*, 226.

34. Gordon and Gilley, "A Trust-Leadership Model," 30.

35. Klaussner, "Trust and Leadership," 427.

36. Kouzes and Posner, *The Leadership Challenge*, 222.

37. Klaussner, "Trust and Leadership," 421–22.

38. "Stephen Covey Quotes," AZquotes, accessed February 4, 2020, https://www.azquotes.com/quote/663806.

39. "Booker T. Washington Quotes," BrainyQuote, accessed February 4, 2020, https://www.brainyquote.com/quotes/booker_t_washington_101736.

40. "Seth Godin Quotes," AZquotes, accessed February 4, 2020, https://www.azquotes.com/quote/1445123.

Chapter 3

1. "Scott Weiss Quotes," BrainyQuote, accessed February 4, 2020, https://www.brainyquote.com/quotes/scott_weiss_687911.

2. *American Heritage Dictionary,* 5th ed. (2011), s.v. "Health."

3. *American Heritage Dictionary,* 5th ed. (2011), s.v. "Healthcare."

4. Yehuda Baruch et al., "Swearing at Work: The Mixed Outcomes of Profanity," *Journal of Managerial Psychology* 32, no. 2 (2017): 158.

5. Susan Scott, *Fierce Conversations: Achieving Success at Work and in Life One Conversation at a Time* (New York: Berkley Publishing Group, 2004), 187.

6. Winston Churchill Quotation," QuoteTab, accessed April 16, 2020, https://www.quotetab.com/quote/by-winston-churchill/if-two-people-agree-on-everything-one-of-them-is-unnecessary?source=people.

7. Dirk De Clercq, Narongsak Thongpapanl, and Dimo Dimov, "When Good Conflict Gets Better and Bad Conflict Becomes Worse: The Role of Social Capital in the Conflict-Innovation Relationship." *Journal of the Academy of Marketing Science* 37 (2009): 294.

8. Dori Meinert, "Scared Stiff," *HR Magazine*, December 2015/January 2016, 12.

9. Ira Chaleff, *The Courageous Follower: Standing Up to and for Our Leaders* (San Francisco: Berrett-Koehler, 2009), 1–9.

10. Marie-Claire Ross, "11 Insightful Leadership Quotes on Culture," *Trustologie* (blog), August 24, 2015, http://www.trustologie.com.au/2015/08/24/11-insightful-leadership-quotes-on-culture/.

11. Richard Runnels, "50 Leaders' Inspirational Quotes on Employee Engagement and Workplace Culture," *Quantum Workplace,* accessed February 4, 2020, https://www.quantumworkplace.com/50-awesome-employee-engagement-quotes.

12. "James Levine Quotes," BrainyQuotes, accessed February 4, 2020, https://www.brainyquote.com/quotes/james_levine_261931.

13. "Johan Huizinga Quotes," BrainyQuotes, accessed February 4, 2020, https://www.brainyquote.com/quotes/johan_huizinga_397291.

Chapter 4

1. Susan Heathfield, "Inspirational Quotes about Showing Respect at Work," *The Balance Careers*, updated May 7, 2019, https://www.thebalance.com/inspirational-quotes-for-business-and-work-about-respect-1919392.

2. M. Scott Peck, *The Different Drum: Community Making and Peace* (New York: Touchstone, 1987), 13–15.

3. Peck, 1987, *The Different Drum*, 13.

4. Peck, 1987, *The Different Drum*, 14.

5. Paul Meshanko, *The Respect Effect: Using the Science of Neuroleadership to Inspire a More Loyal and Productive Workplace (*New York: McGraw-Hill Education, 2013), xiii–xiv.

6. U.S. Equal Employment Opportunity Commission, "EEOC Releases Fiscal Year 2018 Enforcement and Litigation Data," press release 4-10-19, April 10, 2019, https://www.eeoc.gov/eeoc/newsroom/release/4-10-19.cfm.

7. Meshanko, *The Respect Effect*, xiii.

8. Meshanko, *The Respect Effect*, 11.

9. *American Heritage Dictionary*, 5th ed. (2011), s.v. "Respect."

10. *The Oxford Dictionary of Philosophy*, 3rd ed. (2016), s.v. "Respect."

11. Shane Lopez, *Encyclopedia of Positive Psychology* (Malden, MA: Blackwell Publishing, 2013), 843.

12. Peter Northouse, *Leadership: Theory and Practice* (Thousand Oaks, CA: Sage Publications, 2013), 431.

13. Howard Schultz, *Pour Your Heart Into It* (New York: Hyperion, 1997), 5–6.

14. Mellody Hopson, "Color Blind or Color Brave," Filmed March 2014, TED video, 14:11, https://www.ted.com/talks/mellody_hobson_color_blind_or_color_brave.

15. Monnica Williams, "Colorblind Ideology Is a Form of Racism," *Psychology Today*, December 27, 2011, https://www.psychologytoday.com/blog/culturally-speaking/201112/colorblind-ideology-is-form-racism.

16. Williams, "Colorblind Ideology Is a Form of Racism."

17. Meshanko, *The Respect Effect*, viii.

18. Meshanko, *The Respect Effect*, ix.

19. Hopson, "Color Blind or Color Brave."

20. Williams, "Colorblind Ideology Is a Form of Racism."

21. John Maxwell, *There's No Such Thing as Business Ethics: There's Only One Rule for Making Decisions* (New York: Warner Books, 2003), 23.

22. Paula Caligiuri, *Cultural Agility: Building a Pipeline of Successful Global Professionals* (San Francisco: Jossey-Bass, 2012), 57.

23. Meshanko, *The Respect Effect*, 32.

24. Meshanko, *The Respect Effect*, 35.

25. Meshanko, *The Respect Effect*, 36–41.

26. Kathryn Kaplan, Pamela Mestel, and David L. Feldman, "Creating a Culture of Mutual Respect," *AORN Journal* 91, no. 4 (April 2010): 497.

27. Kaplan, Mestel, and Felman, "Creating a Culture," 498.

28. Kaplan, Mestel, and Felman, "Creating a Culture," 498.

29. Kaplan, Mestel, and Felman, "Creating a Culture," 499.

30. Kaplan, Mestel, and Felman, "Creating a Culture," 503.

31. Graham Haydon, "Respect for Persons and for Cultures as a Basis for National and Global Citizenship," *Journal of Moral Education* 35, no. 4 (December 2006): 469.

32. Haydon, "Respect for Persons," 469–70.

33. V. G. Lokare, "Respect for Cultures, Beliefs and Attitudes: A Way to Better Relationships and Understanding," *Counselling Psychology Quarterly* 5, no. 3 (1992).

34. Eileen Maeso, "As a Leader in a Politically Correct Diverse Workplace, How Do You Establish a Culture of Respect?" *Performance Improvement* 56, no. 3 (March 2017): 28.

35. Maeso, "As a Leader," 31.

36. Heathfield, "Inspirational Quotes about Showing Respect at Work."

37. "Albert Einstein Quotes," GoodReads, accessed February 4, 2020, https://www.goodreads.com/author/quotes/9810.Albert_Einstein.

38. "Jackie Robinson Quotes," BrainyQuote, accessed February 4, 2020, https://www.brainyquote.com/quotes/jackie_robinson_140153.

39. "Mona Sutphen Quotes," BrainyQuote, accessed February 4, 2020, https://www.brainyquote.com/quotes/mona_sutphen_622035.

40. "Laurence Sterne Quotes," BrainyQuote, accessed February 4, 2020, https://www.brainyquote.com/quotes/laurence_sterne_165818.

Chapter 5

1. "Quotes about Corporate Image," Quote Master, accessed February 4, 2020, https://www.quotemaster.org/corporate+image.

2. "Corporate Image," *Inc.*, accessed February, 4, 2020, https://www.inc.com/encyclopedia/corporate-image.html.

3. Eleanor McKenzie, "Differences Between Corporate Image & Identity," *Bizfluent*, September 26, 2017, https://bizfluent.com/list-7605016-differences-between-corporate-image-identity.html.

4. "Corporate Image," *Inc.*

5. Vicky Valet, "The World's Most Reputable Companies 2019," *Forbes*, March 7, 2019, https://www.forbes.com/sites/vickyvalet/2019/03/07/the-worlds-most-reputable-companies-2019/#1c2b095913b6.

6. Jacquelyn Smith, "The World's Most Reputable Companies," *Forbes*, June 7, 2012, https://www.forbes.com/sites/jacquelynsmith/2012/06/07/the-worlds-most-reputable-companies/#5c6b4b804b7d.

7. Will Heilpern, "The World's Top 10 Companies, Ranked by Reputation," *Business Insider*, March 25, 2016, http://www.businessinsider.com/10-most-reputable-companies-in-the-world-2016-3.

8. Karsten Strauss, "The World's Most Reputable Companies in 2017," *Forbes*, February 28, 2017), https://www.forbes.com/sites/karstenstrauss/2017/02/28/the-worlds-most-reputable-companies-in-2017/#58dee4592fe3.

9. Reputation Institute, "Powering the World's Most Reputable Companies: 2018 Global RepTrak®," March 15, 2018, https://cdn2.hubspot.net/hubfs/2963875/_PDF/RepTrak/2018-GlobalRT100-Presentation.pdf?t=1535145221533%20target=, 41; Reputation Institute, "Winning in the New Reputation Economy: 2019 Global RepTrak®," March 7, 2019, https://insights.reputationinstitute.com/homepage/global-reptrak-2019, 51.

10. "Corporate Image," *Inc.*

11. Jim Collins, *Good to Great: Why Some Companies Make the Leap and Others Don't*

(New York: Harper Business, 2001), 54.

12. Jacquelyn Smith, "The World's Most Reputable Companies."

13. Jeffrey Pfeffer and Robert Sutton, *The Knowing-Doing Gap* (Boston: Harvard Business School Press, 2000), 14.

14. Larry Greiner and Flemming Poulfelt, eds., *Management Consulting Today and Tomorrow: Perspectives and Advice from 27 Leading World Experts* (New York: Routledge, 2009), 16.

15. Pfeffer and Sutton, *The Knowing-Doing Gap*, 18–19.

16. Greiner and Poulfelt, *Management Consulting Today and Tomorrow*, 41.

17. Duff Anderson, "4 Customer Experience Quotes That Will Make You a Better Marketer," *iPerceptions* (blog), September 10, 2015, https://www.iperceptions.com/blog/customer-experience-quotes.

18. Andrew Gazdecki, "8 Ways Customer Service Affects Your Business's Bottom Line," Bizness Apps, accessed February 4, 2020, https://www.biznessapps.com/blog/8-ways-customer-service-affects-your-businesss-bottom-line/.

19. Anderson, "4 Customer Experience Quotes."

20. Mark Pernice, "Revolutionizing Customer Service," *Harvard Business Review,* April 2016, https://hbr.org/2016/04/revolutionizing-customer-service.

21. Blake Morgan, "Five Trends Shaping the Future of Customer Experience in 2018," *Forbes*, December 5, 2017, https://www.forbes.com/sites/blakemorgan/2017/12/05/five-trends-shaping-the-future-of-customer-experience-in-2018/.

22. Jamie LaReau, "Toyota Polishes Corporate Image in TV Campaign," *Automotive News*, February 28, 2005, http://www.autonews.com/article/20050228/SUB/502280750/toyota-polishes-corporate-image-in-tv-campaign.

23. Michael Stallard, Jason Pankau, and Katharine Stallard, *Connection Culture: The Competitive Advantage of Shared Identity, Empathy, and Understanding at Work* (Alexandria, VA: ATD Press, 2017), 23.

24. Klann, *Building Character,* vii.

25. Stallard, Pankau, and Stallard, *Connection Culture*, 23.

26. Gene Klann, *Building Character: Strengthening the Heart of Good Leadership* (San Francisco: Wiley, 2007), 7–8.

27. Klann, *Building Character*, 18–20.

28. Klann, *Building Character*, 18.

29. Klann, *Building Character*, 18–19.

30. Klann, *Building Character*, 66.

31. Klann, *Building Character*, 84–85.

32. Klann, *Building Character*, 19.

33. Klann, *Building Character*, 106.

34. Klann, *Building Character*, 19.

35. Klann, *Building Character*, 112.

36. Klann, *Building Character*, 125.

37. Klann, *Building Character*, 19–20.

38. Charles Swindoll Quotes: Attitude," Quoteland, accessed February 4, 2020, http://www.quoteland.com/author/Charles-Swindoll-Quotes/1310/.

39. Lisa McQuerrey, "Importance of Employee Behavior in an Organization," *Houston Chronicle*, updated July 1, 2018, http://work.chron.com/importance-employee-behavior-organization-11019.html.

40. "Warren Buffet Quotes," BrainyQuote, accessed February 4, 2020, https://www.brainyquote.com/quotes/warren_buffett_108887.

41. "Aristotle Quotes," BrainyQuote, accessed February 4, 2020, https://www.brainyquote.com/quotes/aristotle_383912.

42. Anderson, "4 Customer Experience Quotes."

Chapter 6

1. "Adam Grant Quotes," BrainyQuote, accessed February 4, 2020, https://www.brainyquote.com/quotes/adam_grant_834202.

2. Peter Northouse, *Leadership: Theory and Practice* (Thousand Oaks, CA: Sage Publications, 2013), 260.

3. Edgar Schein, *Organizational Culture and Leadership* (San Francisco: Wiley, 2010), ix–x.

4. Ken Hultman and Bill Gellermann, *Balancing Individual and Organizational Values: Walking the Tightrope to Success* (San Francisco: Jossey-Bass/Pfeiffer, 2002), 4.

5. Hultman and Gellermann, *Balancing Individual and Organizational Values*, 5.

6. Neil Snyder, James Dowd, Jr., and Dianne Houghton, *Vision, Values, and Courage: Leadership for Quality Management* (New York: Free Press, 1994), 19.

7. Northouse, *Leadership: Theory and Practice*, 259.

8. Gene Klann, *Building Character: Strengthening the Heart of Good Leadership* (San Francisco: Wiley, 2006), 13.

9. James Kouzes and Barry Posner, *The Leadership Challenge* (San Francisco: Jossey-Bass, 2012), 49.

10. Kouzes and Posner, *The Leadership Challenge*, 48.

11. Northouse, *Leadership: Theory and Practice*, 259.

12. Kouzes and Posner, *The Leadership Challenge*, 45–46.

13. Klann, *Building Character*, 121.

14. Kim Cameron and Robert Quinn, *Diagnosing and Changing Organizational Culture: Based On the Competing Values Framework* (San Francisco: Jossey-Bass, 2011), 135–39.

15. Virginia Byrd, "Work Life Values of Four Generations," *Career Planning and Adult Development Journal* 24, no. 3 (Fall 2008): 10–13.

16. Klann, *Building Character*, 13.

17. Klann, *Building Character*, 15.

18. Byrd, "Work Life Values."

19. Lisa Huetteman and Michael Dowling, *The Value of Core Values: Five Keys to Success through Values-Centered Leadership* (Valrico: BookLocker, 2012), 21.

20. Eric Flamholtz and Yvonne Randle, *Corporate Culture: The Ultimate Strategic Asset* (Redwood City, CA: Stanford University Press), 2011, 50.

21. Huetteman and Dowling, *The Value of Core Values*, 67.

22. Klann, *Building Character*, 114.

23. Huetteman and Dowling, *The Value of Core Values*, 68.

24. Klann, *Building Character*, 115.

25. Flamholtz and Randle, *Corporate Culture*, 50.

26. *The Hutchinson Unabridged Encyclopedia with Atlas and Weather Guide* (2016), s.v. "Core Values."

27. Klann, *Building Character*, 112.

28. Snyder, Dowd, and Houghton, *Vision, Values, and Courage*, 22.

29. Snyder, Dowd, and Houghton, *Vision, Values, and Courage*, 22–23.

30. Snyder, Dowd, and Houghton, *Vision, Values, and Courage*, 153.

31. Hultman and Gellermann, *Balancing Individual and Organizational Values*, 30.

32. Klann, *Building Character*, 113.

33. Kouzes and Posner, *The Leadership Challenge*, 94.

34. Flamholtz and Randle, *Corporate Culture*, 50.

35. Klann, *Building Character*, 112.

36. Klann, *Building Character*, 95.

37. John Maxwell, *Intentional Living: Choosing a Life That Matters* (New York: Center Street, 2015), 193.

38. Klann, *Building Character*, 114.

39. Snyder, Dowd, and Houghton, *Vision, Values, and Courage*, 23.

40. Flamholtz and Randle, *Corporate Culture*, 71.

41. Flamholtz and Randle, *Corporate Culture*, 106–07.

42. Victor Lipman, "66% of Employees Would Quit If They Feel Unappreciated," *Forbes*, April 15, 2017, https://www.forbes.com/sites/victorlipman/2017/04/15/66-of-employees-would-quit-if-they-feel-unappreciated/#4ab4a28a6897.

43. Richard Burton, Borge Obel, and Dorthe Hakonsson, *Organizational Design: A Step-by-Step Approach* (Cambridge: Cambridge University Press, 2015), 217.

44. Gary Chapman and Paul White, *The 5 Languages of Appreciation in the Workplace: Empowering Organizations by Encouraging People* (Chicago: Northfield Publishing, 2011), 18, 21–27.

45. Chapman and White, *The 5 Languages of Appreciation*, 45–52, 59–62, 73–77, 83–91, 93–102.

46. Chapman and White, *The 5 Languages of Appreciation*, 99.

47. Chapman and White, *The 5 Languages of Appreciation*, 41.

48. Huetteman and Dowling, *The Value of Core Values*, 27.

49. "Roy E. Disney Quotes," BrainyQuote, accessed February 4, 2020, https://www.brainyquote.com/quotes/roy_e_disney_183365

50. "Michelle Obama Quotes," BrainyQuote, accessed February 4, 2020, https://www.brainyquote.com/quotes/michelle_obama_791345.

51. "Brian Tracy Quotes," BrainyQuote, accessed February 4, 2020, https://www.brainyquote.com/quotes/brian_tracy_132982.

52. "William Arthur Ward Quotes," BrainyQuote, accessed February 4, 2020, https://www.brainyquote.com/quotes/william_arthur_ward_105516.

53. Chapman and White, *The 5 Languages of Appreciation*, 24.

Chapter 7

1. Jane Taylor, "20 Quotes to Inspire Responsibility," *Habits for Wellbeing* (blog), accessed February 4, 2020, https://www.habitsforwellbeing.com /20-quotes-to-inspire-responsibility.

2. John Maxwell, *There's No Such Thing as Business Ethics: There's Only One Rule for Making Decisions* (New York: Warner Books, 2003), xi–3.

3. Peter Northouse, *Leadership: Theory and Practice* (Thousand Oaks, CA: Sage Publications, 2013), 424.

4. Joanne Ciulla, *Ethics, the Heart of Leadership* (Santa Barbara, CA: Praeger, 2014), xv.

5. Gillian Flynn, "Make Employee Ethics Your Business," *Personnel Journal* 74, no. 6 (June 1995): 31.

6. James Kouzes and Barry Posner, *The Leadership Challenge* (San Francisco: Jossey-Bass, 2012), 219–23.

7. Dave Ulrich and Norm Smallwood, "Personal Leader Brand," *Leadership Excellence* 28, no. 4 (2011): 16–17.

8. "Your Personal Brand: A Consistent, Respected Leader," *Miami Examiner*, September 28, 2014.

9. Kouzes and Posner, *The Leadership Challenge*, 16.

10. John Baldoni, *Lead by Example: 50 Ways Great Leaders Inspire Results* (New York: American Management Association, 2009), 3.

11. Joseph Badaracco, *Defining Moments: When Managers Must Choose Between Right and Right* (Boston: Harvard Business Review Press, 1997), 5.

12. Max Bazerman and Ann Tenbrunsel, *Blind Spots: Why We Fail to Do What's Right and What to Do about It* (Princeton, NJ: Princeton University Press, 2011), 70–71.

13. Bazerman and Tenbrunsel, *Blind Spots*, 153.

14. Bazerman and Tenbrunsel, *Blind Spots*, 159.

15. Northouse, *Leadership: Theory and Practice*, 430.

16. Northouse, *Leadership: Theory and Practice*, 434.

17. Paula Caligiuri, *Cultural Agility: Building a Pipeline of Successful Global Professionals* (San Francisco: Jossey-Bass, 2012), 59.

18. Northouse, *Leadership: Theory and Practice*, 435.

19. Craig Johnson, *Organizational Ethics: A Practical Approach* (Thousand Oaks, CA: Sage Publications, 2012), 284.

20. Caligiuri, *Cultural Agility*, 57.

21. Ira Chaleff, *The Courageous Follower: Standing Up to and for Our Leaders* (San Francisco: Berrett-Koehler, 2009), 1–9.

22. Chaleff, *The Courageous Follower*, 1–9.

23. Flynn, "Make Employee Ethics Your Business," 31.

24. Craig Johnson, *Ethics in the Workplace: Tools and Tactics for Organizational Transformation* (Thousand Oaks, CA: Sage Publications, 2007), 234.

25. Flynn, "Make Employee Ethics Your Business," 31–37.

26. Flynn, "Make Employee Ethics Your Business," 31.

27. Craig VanSandt and Christopher Neck, "Bridging Ethics and Self Leadership: Overcoming Ethical Discrepancies between Employee and Organizational Standards," *Journal of Business Ethics* 43, no. 4 (2003): 367.

28. VanSandt and Neck, "Bridging Ethics and Self Leadership," 367.

29. Crane and Matten, *Business Ethics*, 192–93.

30. Flynn, "Make Employee Ethics Your Business," 33.

31. Crane and Matten, *Business Ethics*, 194–95.

32. Flynn, "Make Employee Ethics Your Business," 37.

33. Andrew Crane and Dirk Matten, *Business Ethics: Managing Corporate Citizenship and Sustainability in the Age of Globalization* (Oxford: Oxford University Press, 2010), 11.

34. Johnson, *Ethics in the Workplace*, 328.

35. Johnson, *Ethics in the Workplace*, 328.

36. Bazerman and Tenbrunsel, *Blind Spots*, 160–161.

37. Johnson, *Ethics in the Workplace*, 328.

38. Bazerman and Tenbrunsel, *Blind Spots*, 4.

39. Bazerman and Tenbrunsel, *Blind Spots*, 5.

40. Flynn, "Make Employee Ethics Your Business," 36.

41. Flynn, "Make Employee Ethics Your Business," 37.

42. Ciulla, *Ethics*, 56.

43. Flynn, "Make Employee Ethics Your Business," 37.

44. Chaleff, *The Courageous Follower*, 20–22.

45. "Potter Stewart Quotes," accessed February 4, 2020, https://www.brainyquote.com/quotes/potter_stewart_390058.

46. "Rodney Davis Quotes," QuoteHD, accessed February 4, 2020, http://www.quotehd.com/quotes/rodney-davis-quote-if-youre-guided-by-a-spirit-of-transparency-it-forc.

47. "Albert Camus Quotes," BrainyQuote, accessed February 4, 2020, https://www.brainyquote.com/quotes/albert_camus_121575.

48. "Spencer Johnson Quotes," accessed February 4, 2020, https://www.goodreads.com/quotes/23477-integrity-is-telling-myself-the-truth-and-honesty-is-telling.

49. Frank Bucaro, *Trust Me! Insights into Ethical Leadership* (FCB & Associates, Inc., 2004), 13.

Chapter 8

1. "Mattie Stefanik Quotes," BrainyQuote, accessed February 4, 2020, https://www.brainyquote.com/quotes/mattie_stepanek_319300.

2. Jeanne Meister and Karie Willyerd, *The 2020 Workplace: How Innovative Companies Attract, Develop, and Keep Tomorrow's Employees Today* (New York: HarperCollins Publishers, 2010), 23.

3. Meister and Willyerd, *The 2020 Workplace*, 16.

4. Richard Fry, "Millennials Surpass Gen Xers as the Largest Generation in U.S. Labor Force," *Pew Research Center,* May 11, 2015, http://www.pewresearch.org/fact-tank/2015/05/11/millennials-surpass-gen-xers-as-the-largest-generation-in-u-s-labor-force/.

5. Meister and Willyerd, *The 2020 Workplace*, 20–21.

6. Jacob Morgan, *The Future of Work: Attract New Talent, Build Better Leaders, and Create a Competitive Organization* (Hoboken, NJ: Wiley, 2014), 4.

7. Richard Daft, *The Leadership Experience*, 6th ed. (Stamford, CT: Cengage Learning, 2015), 301.

8. Morgan, *The Future of Work*, 61.

9. Meister and Willyerd, *The 2020 Workplace*, 189.

10. Paula Caligiuri, *Cultural Agility: Building a Pipeline of Successful Global Professionals* (San Francisco: Jossey-Bass, 2012), 17–18, 47, 59.

11. Robert Lussier and Christopher Achua, *Leadership: Theory, Application, & Skill Development*, 5th ed. (Mason, OH: Thomson Higher Education, 2013), 286.

12. Daft, *The Leadership Experience*, 302.

13. Lussier and Achua, *Leadership: Theory, Application, & Skill Development*, 281.

14. Morgan, *The Future of Work*, 8.

15. Yves Doz and Keeley Wilson, *Managing Global Innovation: Frameworks for Integrating Capabilities around the World*, Boston: Harvard Business Review Press, 2012, 127.

16. Losey, Meisinger, and Ulrich, *The Future of Human Resource Management*, 305.

17. Losey, Meisinger, and Ulrich, *The Future of Human Resource Management*, 310.

18. Losey, Meisinger, and Ulrich, *The Future of Human Resource Management*, 309–10.

19. Lussier and Achua, *Leadership: Theory, Application, & Skill Development*, 210–12.

20. Lussier and Achua, *Leadership: Theory, Application, & Skill Development*, 210–12.

21. John Lincoln, "17 Inspirational Quotes to Instantly Foster Teamwork When Unity Is Lost," *Entrepreneur*, June 6, 2019, https://www.entrepreneur.com/article/269941.

22. "Helen Keller Quotes," BrainyQuote, accessed February 4, 2020, https://www.brainyquote.com/quotes/helen_keller_382259.

23. "Robert Orben Quotes," BrainyQuote, accessed February 4, 2020, https://www.brainyquote.com/quotes/robert_orben_159379.

Chapter 9

1. "Brian Tracey Quotes," Goodreads, accessed February 4, 2020, https://www.goodreads.com/quotes/524089-those-people-who-develop-the-ability-to-continuously-acquire-new.

2. Jeffrey Pfeffer and Robert Sutton, *The Knowing-Doing Gap* (Boston: Harvard Business School Press, 2000), 4.

3. "Business Books," Amazon, accessed November 11, 2019, https://www.amazon.com/s?k=business+books&i=stripbooks&ref=nb_sb_noss_1

4. Statista, "Market Size of the Global Workplace Training Industry from 2007 to 2018," Statista, September 12, 2019, https://www.statista.com/statistics/738399/size-of-the-global-workplace-training-market/.

5. Statista, "Management Consulting Market Size by Sector from 2011 to 2020 (in Billion U.S. Dollars)," Statista, September 20, 2019, https://www.statista.com/statistics/466460/global-management-consulting-market-size-by-sector/.

6. Bruce Winston and Kathleen Patterson, "An Integrative Definition of Leadership," *International Journal of Leadership Studies* 1, no. 2 (2006): 8–12.

7. Michael Marquardt, *Building the Learning Organization: Achieving Strategic Advantage through a Commitment to Learning* (Boston: Nicholas Briley Publishing, 2011), 1–2.

8. Marquardt, *Building the Learning Organization*, 12.

9. Diane Wiater, "Transformational Leadership: An Examination of Significant Leadership Development Life Experiences of Selected Doctor of Ministry Students," *ProQuest Dissertations Publishing* (June 2001), 2.

10. Margot Shetterly, *Hidden Figures: The American Dream and the Untold Story of the Black Women Mathematicians Who Helped Win the Space Race* (New York: William Morrow, 2016), 138–39, 167, 171–72, 205–6.

11. Marquardt, *Building the Learning Organization*, ix.

12. Marquardt, *Building the Learning Organization*, 61.

13. Paula Caligiuri, *Cultural Agility: Building a Pipeline of Successful Global Professionals* (San Francisco: Jossey-Bass, 2012), 60–61.

14. Jeanne Meister and Karie Willyerd, *The 2020 Workplace: How Innovative Companies Attract, Develop, and Keep Tomorrow's Employees Today* (New York: HarperCollins Publishers, 2010), 128–30, 183.

15. Marquardt, *Building the Learning Organization*, 2.

16. Peter Senge, *The Fifth Discipline Fieldbook: Strategies and Tools for Building a Learning Organization* (New York: Crown Business, 1994), 221–22.

17. Mike Losey, Sue Meisinger, and Dave Ulrich, *The Future of Human Resource Management: 64 Thought Leaders Explore the Critical HR Issues of Today and Tomorrow* (Hoboken, NJ: Wiley, 2005), 110–18.

18. Ellen Velsor, Cynthia McCauley, and Marian Ruderman, *The Center for Creative Leadership Handbook of Leadership Development* (San Francisco: Jossey-Bass, 2010), 153–75.

19. Michael Watkins, *The First 90 Days: Critical Success Strategies for New Leaders at All Levels* (Boston: Harvard Business School Press, 2003), 17–21.

20. Peter Northouse, *Leadership: Theory and Practice* (Thousand Oaks: Sage Publications, 2013), 44–48.

21. "Denis Waitley Quotes," BrainyQuote, accessed February 4, 2020, https://www.brainyquote.com/quotes/denis_waitley_146933.

22. "Henry Ford Quotes," BrainyQuote, accessed February 4, 2020, https://www.brainyquote.com/quotes/henry_ford_103927.

23. "Rasheed Ogunlaru Quotes," Goodreads, accessed on February 4, 2020, https://www.goodreads.com/quotes/7222519-it-s-essential-to-keep-moving-learning-and-evolving-for-as.

24. "Barack Obama Quotes," BrainyQuote, accessed March 15, 2020, https://www.brainyquote.com/quotes/barack_obama_168695.

Chapter 10

1. Taylor, Jane, "20 Quotes to Inspire Responsibility," *Habits for Wellbeing*, https://www.habitsforwellbeing.com/20-quotes-to-inspire-responsibility/.

2. Thomas Davenport, Jeanne Harris, and Robert Morison, *Analytics at Work: Smarter Decisions, Better Results* (Boston: Harvard Business Review Press, 2010), 118.

3. Alistair Croll and Benjamin Yoskovitz, *Lean Analytics* (Sebastopol, CA: O'Reilly Media, 2013), 389–92.

4. Davenport, Harris, and Morison, *Analytics at Work*, 137–41.

5. Davenport, Harris, and Morison, *Analytics at Work*, 140–41.

6. Peter Smith and Meenakshi Sharma, "Developing Personal Responsibility and Leadership Traits in All Your Employees: Part 1 - Shaping and Harmonizing The High-Performance Drivers," *Management Decision* 40, no. 8 (2002): 767.

7. Di Worrall, *Accountability Leadership: How Great Leaders Build a High Performance Culture of Accountability and Responsibility* (Carlton, NSW, Australia: Di Worrall, 2013), 45.

8. Worrall, *Accountability Leadership*, 48.

9. Peter Smith and Meenakshi Sharma, "Developing Personal Responsibility and Leadership Traits in All Your Employees: Part 2 - Optimally Shaping and Harmonizing Focus, Will and Capability," *Management Decision* 40, no. 9 (2002): 820.

10. Robert Lussier and Christopher Achua, *Leadership: Theory, Application & Skill Development*, 5th ed. (Mason, OH: Cengage Learning, 2013), 338.

11. Gary Burnison, *No Fear of Failure: Real Stories of How Leaders Deal with Risk and Change* (San Francisco: Jossey-Bass, 2011), 115.

12. Burnison, *No Fear of Failure*, 118.

13. Jeffrey Pfeffer and Robert Sutton, *The Knowing-Doing Gap* (Boston: Harvard Business School Press, 2000), 110.

14. Pfeffer and Sutton, *The Knowing-Doing Gap*, 118.

15. Jeanne Meister and Karie Willyerd, *The 2020 Workplace: How Innovative Companies Attract, Develop, and Keep Tomorrow's Employees Today* (New York: HarperCollins Publishers, 2010), 227.

16. Meister and Willyerd, *The 2020 Workplace*, 86.

17. Meister and Willyerd, *The 2020 Workplace*, 238.

18. Meister and Willyerd, *The 2020 Workplace*, 227.

19. Meister and Willyerd, *The 2020 Workplace*, 238.

20. Meister and Willyerd, *The 2020 Workplace*, 227.

21. Douglas Hubbard, *How to Measure Anything* (Hoboken, NJ: Wiley, 2014), 9.

22. Pfeffer and Sutton, *The Knowing-Doing Gap*, 15, 27.

23. Croll and Yoskovitz, *Lean Analytics*, 9.

24. Croll and Yoskovitz, *Lean Analytics*, 37–59, 390.

25. Tim Richardson, *The Responsible Leader: Developing a Culture of Responsibility in an Uncertain World* (Philadelphia: Kogan Page, 2015), 134.

26. Richardson, *The Responsible Leader*, 138–39.

27. Richardson, *The Responsible Leader*, 140.

28. Richardson, *The Responsible Leader*, 135.

29. Richardson, *The Responsible Leader*, 141.

30. Richardson, *The Responsible Leader*, 148.

31. Richardson, *The Responsible Leader*, 160.

32. Richardson, *The Responsible Leader*, 160.

33. Richardson, *The Responsible Leader*, 140.

34. "Jay Samit Quotes," BrainyQuote, accessed February 4, 2020, https://www.brainyquote.com/quotes/jay_samit_747565.

35. "Shiv Khera Quotes," BrainyQuote, accessed February 4, 2020, https://www.brainyquote.com/quotes/shiv_khera_572334.

36. "John C. Maxwell Quotes," AZquotes, accessed February 4, 2020, https://www.azquotes.com/quote/649491.

37. "Jack Welch Quotes," BrainyQuote, accessed February 4, 2020, https://www.brainyquote.com/quotes/jack_welch_458942.

38. "Winston S. Churchill Quotes," Goodreads, accessed March 14, 2020, https://www.goodreads.com/quotes/108654-however-beautiful-the-strategy-you-should-occasionally-look-at-the.

Chapter 11

1. "Steve Jobs Quotes," BrainyQuote, accessed February 4, 2020, https://www.brainyquote.com/quotes/steve_jobs_173474

2. *American Heritage Dictionary*, 5th ed. (2011), s.v. "Care."

3. Edgar Schein, *Organizational Culture and Leadership* (San Francisco: Wiley, 2010), 3.

4. Tony Davila, Marc Epstein, and Robert Shelton, *Making Innovation Work: How to Manage It, Measure It, and Profit from It* (Upper Saddle River, NJ: FT Press, 2013), 59.

5. Jeffrey Phillips, *Relentless Innovation* (New York: McGraw-Hill, 2012), xvii.

6. Gary Oster, *The Light Prize: Perspectives on Christian Innovation* (Virginia Beach, VA: Positive Signs Media, 2011), 161–63.

7. Michael Schrage, *The Innovators' Hypothesis* (Cambridge, MA: MIT Press, 2014), 144.

8. Phillips, *Relentless Innovation*, 58.

9. Michael Ringel et al., "The Most Innovative Companies 2019: The Rise of AI, Platforms, and Ecosystems," Boston Consulting Group, March 2019, http://image-src.bcg.com/Images/BCG-Most-Innovative-Companies-Mar-2019-R2_tcm9-215836.pdf, 4.

10. Scott Berkun, *The Myths of Innovation* (Sebastopol, CA: O'Reilly Media, 2010), 76–79.

11. Berkun, *The Myths of Innovation*, 79.

12. Tim Brown, *Change by Design* (New York: Harper Business, 2009), 26–38.

13. Michael Schrage, *Serious Play* (Boston: Harvard Business School Press, 2000), 89.

14. Davila, Epstein, and Shelton, *Making Innovation Work*, 261.

15. Berkun, *The Myths of Innovation*, 161–62.

16. Davila, Epstein, and Shelton, *Making Innovation Work*, 23–24.

17. Phillips, *Relentless Innovation*, 59.

18. Michael Marquardt, *Building the Learning Organization: Achieving Strategic Advantage through a Commitment to Learning* (Boston: Nicholas Briley Publishing, 2011), 129–30.

19. Davila, Epstein, and Shelton, *Making Innovation Work*, 211–14, 228–29.

20. Pagan Kennedy, *Inventology: How We Dream Up Things that Change the World* (New York: Houghton Mifflin Harcourt, 2016), 29–30.

21. Brown, *Change by Design*, 39–62.

22. Marquardt, *Building the Learning Organization*, 140–54.

23. Davila, Epstein and Shelton, *Making Innovation Work*, 211–24.

24. Michael Michalko, *Thinkertoys: A Handbook of Business Creativity* (Berkeley, CA: Ten Speed Press, 2006), 22–34.

25. Vijay Kumar, Vijay. *101 Design Methods* (Hoboken: Wiley & Sons, 2013), 90.

26. Schrage, *Serious Play*, 19.

27. Schrage, *Serious Play*, 18–19.

28. Dorothy Leonard, *Wellsprings of Knowledge* (Boston: Harvard Business School Press, 1998), 125–27.

29. Phillips, *Relentless Innovation*, 64–68.

30. Davila, Epstein, and Shelton, *Making Innovation Work*, 181–87.

31. Davila, Epstein, andShelton, *Making Innovation Work*, 258–60.

32. Berkun, *The Myths of Innovation*, xv.

33. Berkun, *The Myths of Innovation*, 35.

34. "Steven Johnson Quotes," BrainyQuote, accessed February 4, 2020, https://www.brainyquote.com/quotes/steven_johnson_527620.

35. "Margaret Heffernan Quotes," BrainyQuote, accessed February 4, 2020, https://www.brainyquote.com/quotes/margaret_heffernan_556959.

36. Peter Manzo, "Fail Faster, Succeed Sooner," *Stanford Social Innovation Review*, September 23, 2008, https://ssir.org/articles/entry/fail_faster_succeed_sooner.

Chapter 12

1. "George Washington Carver Quotes," BrainyQuote, accessed February 4, 2020, https://www.brainyquote.com/quotes/george_washington_carver_158551.

2. Nina Zipkin, "8 Far-Out 'Jetsons' Contraptions That Actually Exist Today," *Entrepreneur*, April 17, 2015, https://www.entrepreneur.com/article/245192.

3. Gerinda Jooste, "Great Leaders = A Vision for Success," *Accountancy SA*, July 2016, 4.

4. Neil Snyder, James Dowd, Jr., and Dianne Houghton, *Vision, Values, and Courage: Leadership for Quality Management* (New York: Free Press, 1994), 73.

5. Pat Williams and Jim Denney, *Leadership Excellence: The Seven Sides of Leadership for the 21st Century* (Uhrichsville, OH: Barbour Publishing, 2012), 37–39.

6. Williams and Denney, *Leadership Excellence*, 41–42.

7. Snyder, Dowd, and Houghton, *Vision, Values, and Courage*, 73.

8. Snyder, Dowd, and Houghton, *Vision, Values, and Courage*, 73; James Kouzes and Barry Posner, *The Leadership Challenge* (San Francisco: Jossey-Bass, 2012), 156.

9. Snyder, Dowd, and Houghton, *Vision, Values, and Courage*, 77–78.

10. Williams and Denney, *Leadership Excellence*, 58.

11. Snyder, Dowd, and Houghton, *Vision, Values, and Courage*, 84.

12. Jacob Morgan, *The Future of Work: Attract New Talent, Build Better Leaders, and Create a Competitive Organization* (Hoboken, NJ: Wiley, 2014), 208.

13. Kouzes and Posner, *The Leadership Challenge*, 143–44.

14. Kouzes and Posner, *The Leadership Challenge*, 147–50.

15. Morgan, *The Future of Work*, 209.

16. Snyder, Dowd, and Houghton, *Vision, Values, and Courage*, 85.

17. Richard Hughes, Katherine Beatty, and David Dinwoodie, *Becoming a Strategic Leader: Your Role in Your Organization's Enduring Success* (San Francisco: Jossey-Bass, 2014), 3–4, 9–50.

18. Hughes, Beatty, and Dinwoodie, *Becoming a Strategic Leader*, 55, 105, 148.

19. Hughes, Beatty, and Dinwoodie, *Becoming a Strategic Leader*, 11.

20. Ackermann and Eden, *Making Strategy*, 5.

21. Thomas Chermack, *Scenario Planning in Organizations: How to Create, Use, and Assess Scenarios* (San Francisco: Berrett-Koehler, 2011), 1–2.

22. Hughes, Beatty, and Dinwoodie, *Becoming a Strategic Leader*, 4.

23. Ackerman and Eden, *Making Strategy*, 27.

24. Bruce Winston and Kathleen Patterson, "An Integrative Definition of Leadership," *International Journal of Leadership Studies* 1, no. 2 (2006): 20.

25. Hughes, Beatty, and Dinwoodie, *Becoming a Strategic Leader*, 68.

26. Chermack, *Scenario Planning in Organizations*, 107–10.

27. "STEEPLE," MBA Skool, accessed February 4, 2020, https://www.mbaskool.com/business-concepts/marketing-and-strategy-terms/6814-steeple.html.

28. Chermack, *Scenario Planning in Organizations*, 103–05.

29. Zorica Srdjevic, Ratko Bajcetic, and Bojan Srdjevic, "Identifying the Criteria Set for Multi-Criteria Decision Making Based on SWOT/PESTLE Analysis: A Case Study of Reconstructing a Water Intake Structure," *Water Resources Management* 26, no. 12 (May 2012): 3385.

30. Pagan Kennedy, *Inventology: How We Dream Up Things that Change the World* (New York: Houghton Mifflin Harcourt, 2016), 30.

31. Hughes, Beatty, and Dinwoodie, *Becoming a Strategic Leader*, 106.

32. Hughes, Beatty, and Dinwoodie, *Becoming a Strategic Leader*, 106.

33. Hughes, Beatty, and Dinwoodie, *Becoming a Strategic Leader*, 145–95.

34. Tony Davila, Marc Epstein, and Robert Shelton, *Making Innovation Work: How to Manage It, Measure It, and Profit from It* (Upper Saddle River, NJ: FT Press, 2013), 10–12.

35. Hughes, Beatty, and Dinwoodie, *Becoming a Strategic Leader*, 1–4, 107–19.

36. Hughes, Beatty, and Dinwoodie, *Becoming a Strategic Leader*, 9–50.

37. Edward Cornish, *Futuring: The Exploration of the Future* (Bethesda, MD: World Future Society, 2004), 293.

38. Cornish, *Futuring*, 3–4.

39. Cornish, *Futuring*, 4.

40. Andy Hines, "Strategic Foresight: State of the Art," *The Futurist,* September–October 2016, 18.

41. Michael McKinney, "Quotes on VISION," Leadership Now, accessed February 4, 2020, https://www.leadershipnow.com/visionquotes.html.

42. "Lifelong Learning Quotes," Goodreads, accessed February 4, 2020, https://www.goodreads.com/quotes/tag/lifelong-learning.

43. "Tony Dungy Quotes," Goodreads, accessed February 4, 2020, https://www.goodreads.com/quotes/73492-the-first-step-toward-creating-an-improved-future-is-developing.

Chapter 13

1. "John Rampton Quotes," BrainyQuote, accessed February 4, 2020, https://www.brainyquote.com/quotes/john_rampton_799442

2. Jeanne Meister and Karie Willyerd, *The 2020 Workplace: How Innovative Companies Attract, Develop, and Keep Tomorrow's Employees Today* (New York: HarperCollins Publishers, 2010), 187.

3. Richard Daft, *The Leadership Experience*, 6th ed. (Stamford, CT: Cengage Learning, 2015), 241.

4. Bernard Bass and Ruth Bass, *The Bass Handbook of Leadership: Theory, Research, and Managerial Applications*, 4th ed. (New York: Free Press, 2008), 305.

5. Exod 18:17–27.

6. Bass and Bass, *The Bass Handbook of Leadership*, 306.

7. Daft, *The Leadership Experience*, 241.

8. Bass and Bass, *The Bass Handbook of Leadership*, 305.

9. Richard Burton, Borge Obel, and Dorthe Hakonsson, *Organizational Design: A Step-by-Step Approach* (Cambridge: Cambridge University Press, 2015), 7.

10. Bass and Bass, *The Bass Handbook of Leadership*, 305.

11. Daft, *The Leadership Experience*, 242–43.

12. Russell Sarder, *Building an Innovative Learning Organization: A Framework to Build a Smarter Workforce, Adapt to Change, and Drive Growth* (Hoboken, NJ: Wiley, 2016), 4–7.

13. Edward Fang et al., "The Impact of New Product & Operations Technological Practices on Organization Structure," *International Journal of Production Economics* 145, no. 2 (2013): 735.

14. Kenneth Kahn, *The PDMA Handbook of New Product Development* (Hoboken, NJ: Wiley, 2013), 45.

15. Kahn, *The PDMA Handbook*, 44.

16. "The Speed of the Leader Determines the Pace of the Pack," All Motivational Quotes, accessed February 4, 2020, http://www.allmotivationalquotes.com/quote/ralph-waldo-emerson-3/.

17. Jacob Morgan, *The Future of Work: Attract New Talent, Build Better Leaders, and Create a Competitive Organization* (Hoboken, NJ: Wiley, 2014), 210.

18. Daft, *The Leadership Experience*, 466.

19. Robert Lussier and Christopher Achua, *Leadership: Theory, Application, & Skill Development*, 5th ed. (Mason, OH: Cengage Learning, 2013), 339.

20. "Servant Leadership Quotes," Triple Crown Leadership, accessed February 4, 2020, http://www.triplecrownleadership.com/assets/Servant-Leadership-Quotes.pdf.

21. Bass and Bass, *The Bass Handbook of Leadership*, 306.

22. Bass and Bass, *The Bass Handbook of Leadership*, 307.

23. "Bill Gates Quotes," BrainyQuote, accessed February 4, 2020, https://www.brainyquote.com/quotes/bill_gates_385136.

24. "Ruth Reichl Quotes," BrainyQuote, accessed February 4, 2020, https://www.brainyquote.com/quotes/ruth_reichl_702205.

25. "Ken Blanchard Quotes," BrainyQuote, accessed February 4, 2020, https://www.brainyquote.com/quotes/ken_blanchard_173324.

Chapter 14

1. "Thrive Quotes," Goodreads, accessed on March 14, 2020, https://www.goodreads.com/quotes/tag/thrive.

2. Mike Losey, Sue Meisinger, and Dave Ulrich, *The Future of Human Resource Management: 64 Thought Leaders Explore the Critical HR Issues of Today and Tomorrow* (Hoboken, NJ: Wiley, 2005), 153.

3. Christopher Dawson, *Leading Culture Change: What Every CEO Needs to Know* (Stanford, CA: Stanford Business Books, 2010), 94–108.

4. Edgar Schein, *Organizational Culture and Leadership* (San Francisco: Wiley, 2010), 305–6.

5. Kim Cameron and Robert Quinn, *Diagnosing and Changing Organizational Culture: Based On the Competing Values Framework* (San Francisco: Jossey-Bass, 2011), 110–11, 115.

6. Christopher Dawson, *Leading Culture Change: What Every CEO Needs to Know* (Stanford, CA: Stanford Business Books, 2010), 94–108.

7. Schein, *Organizational Culture and Leadership*, 107–10.

8. Cameron and Quinn, *Diagnosing and Changing Organizational Culture*, 115.

9. Cameron and Quinn, *Diagnosing and Changing Organizational Culture*, 137–38.

10. Diane Wiater, "Transformational Leadership: An Examination of Significant Leadership Development Life Experiences of Selected Doctor of Ministry Students," *ProQuest Dissertations Publishing* (June 2001), 2.

11. Losey, Meisinger, and Ulrich, *The Future of Human Resource Management*, 153.

12. Cameron and Quinn, *Diagnosing and Changing Organizational Culture*, 19–20.

13. Schein, *Organizational Culture and Leadership*, 18, 23.

14. Cameron and Quinn, *Diagnosing and Changing Organizational Culture*, 1–2.

15. Sonya Snellenberger, "Millennials Reshaping Workplace Culture: Generations Working Together Can Keep Companies Productive," *Journal Gazette*, June 22, 2014, A14–A15.

16. "Barack Obama Quotes," BrainyQuote, accessed March 15, 2020, https://www.brainyquote.com/quotes/barack_obama_409128.

17. "Barbara Bush Quotes," BrainyQuote, accessed February 4, 2020, https://www.brainyquote.com/quotes/barbara_bush_162846.

18. "Sallust Quotes," BrainyQuote, accessed February 4, 2020, https://www.brainyquote.com/quotes/sallust_154910.

19. "Thrive Quotes," Goodreads, accessed February 4, 2020, https://www.goodreads.com/quotes/tag/thrive?page=2.

20. "Rasheed Ogunlaru Quotes, " Goodreads, accessed February 4, 2020, https://www.goodreads.com/quotes/8584829-inspiration-may-come-from-many-places-but-motivation---the.

21. "Maya Angelou Quotes," BrainyQuote, accessed February 4, 2020, https://www.brainyquote.com/quotes/maya_angelou_634520.

References

Ackermann, Fran, and Colin Eden. *Making Strategy: Mapping Out Strategic Success*. Thousand Oaks, CA: Sage Publications, 2011.

Badaracco, Joseph. *Defining Moments: When Managers Must Choose between Right and Right*. Boston: Harvard Business Review Press, 1997.

Baldoni, John. *Lead by Example: 50 Ways Great Leaders Inspire Results*. New York: American Management Association, 2009.

Baruch, Yehuda, Rea Prouska, Ariane Ollier-Malaterre, and Jennifer Bunk. "Swearing at Work: The Mixed Outcomes of Profanity." *Journal of Managerial Psychology* 32, no. 2 (2017): 149–62.

Bass, Bernard, and Ruth Bass. *The Bass Handbook of Leadership: Theory, Research, and Managerial Applications*, 4th ed. New York: Free Press, 2008.

Bazerman, Max, and Ann Tenbrunsel. *Blind Spots: Why We Fail to Do What's Right and What to Do about It*. Princeton, NJ: Princeton University Press, 2011.

Berkun, Scott. *The Myths of Innovation*. Sebastopol, CA: O'Reilly Media, 2010.

Bremer, Marcella. *Organizational Culture Change: Unleashing Your Organization's Potential in Circles of 10*. Zwolle, Netherlands: Kikker Groep, 2012.

Brown, Tim. *Change by Design*. New York: Harper Business, 2009.

Bucaro, Frank. *Trust Me! Insights into Ethical Leadership*. FCB & Associates, 2004.

Burnison, Gary. *No Fear of Failure: Real Stories of How Leaders Deal With Risk and Change*. San Francisco: Jossey-Bass, 2011.

Burton, Richard, Borge Obel, and Dorthe Hakonsson. *Organizational Design: A Step-by-Step Approach*. Cambridge: Cambridge University Press, 2015.

Byrd, Virginia. "Work Life Values of Four Generations." *Career Planning and Adult Development Journal* 24, no. 3 (Fall 2008): 9.

Byrne, Jo-Ann. "A Culture of Trust: Staff Development's Role in Enhancing Organizational Culture." *Strategies for Nurse Managers* (July 2010). 9–11.

Caligiuri, Paula. *Cultural Agility: Building a Pipeline of Successful Global Professionals*. San Francisco: Jossey-Bass, 2012.

Cameron, Kim, and Robert Quinn. *Diagnosing and Changing Organizational Culture: Based On the Competing Values Framework*. San Francisco: Jossey-Bass, 2011.

Chaleff, Ira. *The Courageous Follower: Standing Up to & for Our Leaders*. San Francisco: Berrett-Koehler, 2009.

Chapman, Gary, and Paul White. *The 5 Languages of Appreciation in the Workplace: Empowering Organizations by Encouraging People*. Chicago: Northfield Publishing, 2011.

Chermack, Thomas. *Scenario Planning in Organizations: How to Create, Use, and Assess Scenarios*. San Francisco: Berrett-Koehler, 2011.

Ciulla, Joanne. *Ethics, the Heart of Leadership*. Santa Barbara, CA: Praeger, 2014.

Collins, Jim. *Good to Great: Why Some Companies Make the Leap and Others Don't*. New York: Harper Business, 2001.

Cornish, Edward. *Futuring: The Exploration of the Future*. Bethesda, MD: World Future Society, 2004.

Crane, Andrew, and Dirk Matten. *Business Ethics: Managing Corporate Citizenship and Sustainability in the Age of Globalization*. Oxford: Oxford University Press, 2010.

Croll, Alistair, and Benjamin Yoskovitz. *Lean Analytics*. Sebastopol, CA: O'Reilly Media, 2013.

Daft, Richard. *The Leadership Experience*, 6th ed. Stamford, CT: Cengage Learning, 2015.

Davenport, Thomas, Jeanne Harris, and Robert Morison. *Analytics at Work: Smarter Decisions, Better Results*. Boston: Harvard Business Review Press, 2010.

Davis, Nick. "Executive Coaching Survey Shows Serious Lack of Trust in Leaders." *Davis Associates*. https://davisassociates.co.uk/executive-coaching-builds-trust/?utm_source=enoutreach&utm_medium=article.

Davila, Tony, Marc Epstein, and Robert Shelton. *Making Innovation Work: How to Manage It, Measure It, and Profit from It*. Upper Saddle River, NJ: FT Press, 2013.

Dawson, Christopher. *Leading Culture Change: What Every CEO Needs to Know*. Stanford, CA: Stanford Business Books, 2010.

De Clercq, Dirk, Narongsak Thongpapanl, and Dimo Dimov. "When Good Conflict Gets Better and Bad Conflict Becomes Worse: The Role of Social Capital in the Conflict-Innovation Relationship." *Journal of the Academy of Marketing Science* 37 (2009): 283–97.

Doz, Yves, and Keeley Wilson. *Managing Global Innovation: Frameworks for Integrating Capabilities around the World*. Boston: Harvard Business Review Press, 2012.

Fang, Edward, Qizhi Wu, Chaowei Miao, Jiansheng Xia, and Dezhi Chen. "The Impact of New Product & Operations Technological Practices on Organization Structure." *International Journal of Production Economics* 145, no. 2 (2013): 733–42.

Flamholtz, Eric, and Yvonne Randle. *Corporate Culture: The Ultimate Strategic Asset*. Redwood City, CA: Stanford University Press, 2011.

Flynn, Gillian. "Make Employee Ethics Your Business." *Personnel Journal* 74, no. 6 (June 1995): 30.

Fry, Richard. "Millennials Surpass Gen Xers as the Largest Generation in U.S. Labor Force." *Pew Research Center*, May 11, 2015. http://www.pewresearch.org/fact-tank/2015/05/11/millennials-surpass-gen-xers-as-the-largest-generation-in-u-s-labor-force/.

REFERENCES

Gazdecki, Andrew. "8 Ways Customer Service Affects Your Business's Bottom Line." Bizness Apps, accessed February 4, 2020. https://www.biznessapps.com/blog/8-ways-customer-service-affects-your-businesss-bottom-line/.

Gordon, Gus, and Jerry Gilley. "A Trust-Leadership Model." *Performance Improvement* 51, no. 7 (August 2012): 28–35.

Greiner, Larry, and Flemming Poulfelt, eds. *Management Consulting Today and Tomorrow: Perspectives and Advice from 27 Leading World Experts*. New York: Routledge, 2009.

Haydon, Graham. "Respect for Persons and for Cultures as a Basis for National and Global Citizenship." *Journal of Moral Education* 35, no. 4 (December 2006): 457–71.

Heilpern, Will. "The World's Top 10 Companies, Ranked by Reputation." *Business Insider*, March 25, 2016. http://www.businessinsider.com/10-most-reputable-companies-in-the-world-2016-3.

Hines, Andy. "Strategic Foresight: State of the Art." *The Futurist*, September–October, 2016.

Hopen, Deborah. "Editor's Notebook: Does Culture Eat Strategy?" *The Journal for Quality and Participation* 31, no. 2 (Summer 2008): 3.

Hopson, Mellody. "Color Blind or Color Brave." Filmed March 2014. TED video, 14:11. https://www.ted.com/talks/mellody_hobson_color_blind_or_color_brave.

Hubbard, Douglas. *How to Measure Anything*. Hoboken, NJ: Wiley, 2014.

Huetteman, Lisa, and Michael Dowling. *The Value of Core Values: Five Keys to Success through Values-Centered Leadership*. Valrico, FL: BookLocker, 2012.

Hughes, Richard, Katherine Beatty, and David Dinwoodie. *Becoming a Strategic Leader: Your Role in Your Organization's Enduring Success*. San Francisco: Jossey-Bass, 2014.

Hultman, Ken, and Bill Gellermann. *Balancing Individual and Organizational Values: Walking the Tightrope to Success*. San Francisco: Jossey-Bass/Pfeiffer, 2002.

Johnson, Craig. *Ethics in the Workplace: Tools and Tactics for Organizational Transformation*. Thousand Oaks, CA: Sage Publications, 2007.

———. *Organizational Ethics: A Practical Approach*. Thousand Oaks, CA: Sage Publications, 2012.

Jooste, Gerinda. "Great Leaders = A Vision for Success." *Accountancy SA*, July 2016, 4.

Kahn, Kenneth. *The PDMA Handbook of New Product Development*. Hoboken, NJ: Wiley, 2013.

Kaplan, Kathryn, Pamela Mestel, and David L. Feldman. "Creating a Culture of Mutual Respect." *AORN Journal* 91, no. 4 (April 2010): 495–510.

Kawasaki, Guy, and Michele Moreno. *Rules for Revolutionaries: The Capitalist Manifesto for Creating and Marketing New Products and Services*. New York: HarperCollins, 2000.

Kennedy, Pagan. *Inventology: How We Dream Up Things that Change the World*. New York: Houghton Mifflin Harcourt, 2016.

Klann, Gene. *Building Character: Strengthening the Heart of Good Leadership*. San Francisco: Wiley, 2006.

Klaussner, Stefan. "Trust and Leadership: Toward an Interactive Perspective." *Journal of Change Management* 12, no. 4 (December 2012): 417–39.

Kouzes, James, and Barry Posner. *The Leadership Challenge*. San Francisco: Jossey-Bass, 2012.

Kumar, Vijay. *101 Design Methods*. Hoboken, NJ: Wiley, 2013.

LaReau, Jamie. "Toyota Polishes Corporate Image in TV Campaign." *Automotive News*, February 28, 2005. http://www.autonews.com/article/20050228/SUB/502280750/toyota-polishes-corporate-image-in-tv-campaign.

Leonard, Dorothy. *Wellsprings of Knowledge*. Boston: Harvard Business School Press, 1998.

Lipman, Victor. "66% of Employees Would Quit If They Feel Unappreciated." *Forbes*, April 15, 2017. https://www.forbes.com/sites/victorlipman/2017/04/15/66-of-employees-would-quit-if-they-feel-unappreciated/#4ab4a28a6897.

Lokare, V. G. "Respect for Cultures, Beliefs and Attitudes: A Way to Better Relationships and Understanding." *Counselling Psychology Quarterly* 5, no. 3 (1992): 227–29.

Lopez, Shane. *Encyclopedia of Positive Psychology*. Malden, MA: Blackwell Publishing, 2013.

Losey, Mike, Sue Meisinger, and Dave Ulrich. *The Future of Human Resource Management: 64 Thought Leaders Explore the Critical HR Issues of Today and Tomorrow*. Hoboken, NJ: Wiley, 2005.

Lussier, Robert, and Christopher Achua. *Leadership: Theory, Application, & Skill Development*, 5th ed. Mason, OH: Cengage Learning, 2013.

Maeso, Eileen. "As a Leader in a Politically Correct Diverse Workplace, How Do You Establish a Culture of Respect?" *Performance Improvement* 56, no. 3 (March 2017): 28–32.

Maister, David, Charles Green, and Robert Galford. *The Trusted Advisor*. New York: Simon & Schuster, 2001.

Manzo, Peter. "Fail Faster, Succeed Sooner." *Stanford Social Innovation Review*, September 23, 2008. https://ssir.org/articles/entry/fail_faster_succeed_sooner.

Marquardt, Michael. *Building the Learning Organization: Achieving Strategic Advantage through a Commitment to Learning*. Boston: Nicholas Briley Publishing, 2011.

Maxwell, John. *Intentional Living: Choosing a Life That Matters*. New York: Center Street, 2015.

———. *There's No Such Thing as Business Ethics: There's Only One Rule for Making Decisions*. New York: Warner Books, 2003.

McKenzie, Eleanor. "Differences Between Corporate Image & Identity." *Bizfluent*, September 26, 2017. https://bizfluent.com/list-7605016-differences-between-corporate-image-identity.html.

McQuerrey, Lisa. "Importance of Employee Behavior in an Organization." *Houston Chronicle*, July 1, 2018. http://work.chron.com/importance-employee-behavior-organization-11019.html.

REFERENCES

Meinert, Dori. "Scared Stiff." *HR Magazine*, December 2015/January 2016, 12.

Meister, Jeanne, and Karie Willyerd. *The 2020 Workplace: How Innovative Companies Attract, Develop, and Keep Tomorrow's Employees Today*. New York: HarperCollins Publishers, 2010.

Meshanko, Paul. *The Respect Effect: Using the Science of Neuroleadership to Inspire a More Loyal and Productive Workplace*. New York: McGraw-Hill Education, 2013.

Miami Examiner. "Your Personal Brand: A Consistent, Respected Leader." September 28, 2014.

Michalko, Michael. *Thinkertoys: A Handbook of Business Creativity*. Berkeley, CA: Ten Speed Press, 2006.

Morgan, Blake. "Five Trends Shaping the Future of Customer Experience in 2018." *Forbes*, December 5, 2017. HTTPS://WWW.FORBES.COM/SITES/BLAKEMORGAN/2017/12/05/FIVE-TRENDS-SHAPING-THE-FUTURE-OF-CUSTOMER-EXPERIENCE-IN-2018/.

Morgan, Jacob. *The Future of Work: Attract New Talent, Build Better Leaders, and Create a Competitive Organization*. Hoboken, NJ: Wiley, 2014.

Northouse, Peter. *Leadership: Theory and Practice*. Thousand Oaks, CA: Sage Publications, 2013.

Opzeeland, Pascal. "The 8 Customer Service Skills and Traits You Should Look For." *Userlike* (blog), February 23, 2017. https://www.userlike.com/en/blog/customer-service-skills-traits.

Oster, Gary. *The Light Prize: Perspectives on Christian Innovation*. Virginia Beach, VA: Positive Signs Media, 2011.

Peck, M. Scott. *The Different Drum: Community Making and Peace*, New York: Touchstone, 1987.

Pernice, Mark. "Revolutionizing Customer Service." *Harvard Business Review*, April 2016. https://hbr.org/2016/04/revolutionizing-customer-service.

Pfeffer, Jeffrey, and Robert Sutton. *The Knowing-Doing Gap*. Boston: Harvard Business School Press, 2000.

Phillips, Jeffrey. *Relentless Innovation*. New York: McGraw-Hill, 2012.

Reputation Institute. "Powering the World's Most Reputable Companies: 2018 Global RepTrak®." March 15, 2018. https://cdn2.hubspot.net/hubfs/2963875/_PDF/RepTrak/2018-GlobalRT100-Presentation.pdf?t=1535145221533%20target=.

———. "Winning in the New Reputation Economy: 2019 Global RepTrak®." March 7, 2019. https://insights.reputationinstitute.com/homepage/global-reptrak-2019.

Richards, Jay. *Money, Greed, and God*. New York: HarperOne, 2010.

Richardson, Tim. *The Responsible Leader: Developing a Culture of Responsibility in an Uncertain World*. Philadelphia: Kogan Page, 2015.

Ries, Eric. *The Lean Startup: How Today's Entrepreneurs Use Continuous Innovation to Create Radically Successful Businesses*. New York: Crown Business, 2011.

Ringel, Michael, Florian Grassl, Ramón Baeza, Derek Kennedy, Michael Spira, and Justin Manly. "The Most Innovative Companies 2019: The Rise of AI, Platforms, and Ecosystems." Boston Consulting Group, March 2019. http://image-src.bcg.com/Images/BCG-Most-Innovative-Companies-Mar-2019-R2_tcm9-215836.pdf.

Sarder, Russell. *Building an Innovative Learning Organization: A Framework to Build a Smarter Workforce, Adapt to Change, and Drive Growth.* Hoboken, NJ: Wiley, 2016.

Schein, Edgar. *Organizational Culture and Leadership.* San Francisco: Wiley, 2010.

Schrage, Michael. *Serious Play.* Boston: Harvard Business School Press, 2000.

———. *The Innovators' Hypothesis.* Cambridge, MA: MIT Press, 2014.

Schultz, Howard. *Pour Your Heart into It.* New York: Hyperion, 1997.

Scott, Susan. *Fierce Conversations: Achieving Success at Work and in Life One Conversation at a Time.* New York: Berkley Publishing Group, 2004.

Senge, Peter. *The Fifth Discipline Fieldbook: Strategies and Tools for Building a Learning Organization.* New York: Crown Business, 1994.

Shetterly, Margot. *Hidden Figures: The American Dream and the Untold Story of the Black Women Mathematicians Who Helped Win the Space Race.* New York: William Morrow, 2016.

Smith, Jacquelyn. "The World's Most Reputable Companies." *Forbes*, June 7, 2012. https://www.forbes.com/sites/jacquelynsmith/2012/06/07/the-worlds-most-reputable-companies/#5c6b4b804b7d.

Smith, Peter, and Meenakshi Sharma. "Developing Personal Responsibility and Leadership Traits in All Your Employees: Part 1 - Shaping and Harmonizing the High-Performance Drivers." *Management Decision* 40, no. 8 (2002): 764–74.

———. "Developing Personal Responsibility and Leadership Traits in All Your Employees: Part 2 - Optimally Shaping and Harmonizing Focus, Will and Capability." *Management Decision* 40, no. 9 (2002): 814–22.

Snellenberger, Sonya. "Millennials Reshaping Workplace Culture: Generations Working Together Can Keep Companies Productive." *Journal Gazette*, June 22, 2014, A14–A15.

Snyder, Neil, James Dowd, Jr., and Dianne Houghton. *Vision, Values, and Courage: Leadership for Quality Management.* New York: Free Press, 1994.

Srdjevic, Zorica, Ratko Bajcetic, and Bojan Srdjevic. "Identifying the Criteria Set for Multi-Criteria Decision Making Based on SWOT/PESTLE Analysis: A Case Study of Reconstructing a Water Intake Structure." *Water Resources Management* 26, no. 12 (May 2012): 3379–93.

Stallard, Michael, Jason Pankau, and Katharine Stallard. *Connection Culture: The Competitive Advantage of Shared Identity, Empathy, and Understanding at Work.* Alexandria, VA: ATD Press, 2017.

Statista. "Management Consulting Market Size by Sector from 2011 to 2020 (in Billion U.S. Dollars)." Statista, September 20, 2019. https://www.statista.com/statistics/466460/global-management-consulting-market-size-by-sector/

———. "Market Size of the Global Workplace Training Industry from 2007 to 2018." Statista, September 12, 2019. https://www.statista.com/statistics/738399/size-of-the-global-workplace-training-market/.

Strauss, Karsten. "The World's Most Reputable Companies in 2017." *Forbes*, February 28, 2017. https://www.forbes.com/sites/karstenstrauss/2017/02/28/the-worlds-most-reputable-companies-in-2017/#29c01ff32fe3.

Sutherland, Ian. "Learning and Growing: Trust, Leadership, and Response to Crisis." *Journal of Educational Administration* 55, no. 1 (2017): 2–17.

Ulrich, Dave, and Norm Smallwood. "Personal Leader Brand." *Leadership Excellence* 28, no. 4 (2011): 16–17.

U.S. Equal Employment Opportunity Commission. "EEOC Releases Fiscal Year 2018 Enforcement and Litigation Data." Press release 4-10-19, April 10, 2019. https://www.eeoc.gov/eeoc/newsroom/release/4-10-19.cfm.

Valet, Vicky. "The World's Most Reputable Companies 2019." *Forbes*, March 7, 2019. https://www.forbes.com/sites/vickyvalet/2019/03/07/the-worlds-most-reputable-companies-2019/#1c2b095913b6.

VanSandt, Craig, and Christopher Neck. "Bridging Ethics and Self Leadership: Overcoming Ethical Discrepancies between Employee and Organizational Standards." *Journal of Business Ethics* 43, no. 4 (2003): 363–87.

Velsor, Ellen, Cynthia McCauley, and Marian Ruderman. *The Center for Creative Leadership Handbook of Leadership Development*. San Francisco: Jossey-Bass, 2010.

Vesper, Karl. *New Venture Mechanics*. New York: Prentice Hall College Division, 1993.

Watkins, Michael. *The First 90 Days: Critical Success Strategies for New Leaders at All Levels*. Boston: Harvard Business School Press, 2003.

Wiater, Diane. "Transformational Leadership: An Examination of Significant Leadership Development Life Experiences of Selected Doctor of Ministry Students." *ProQuest Dissertations Publishing* (June 2001).

Williams, Monnica. "Colorblind Ideology Is a Form of Racism." *Psychology Today*, December 27, 2011. https://www.psychologytoday.com/blog/culturally-speaking/201112/colorblind-ideology-is-form-racism.

Williams, Pat, and Jim Denney. *Leadership Excellence: The Seven Sides of Leadership for the 21st Century*. Uhrichsville, OH: Barbour Publishing, 2012.

Winston, Bruce, and Kathleen Patterson. "An Integrative Definition of Leadership." *International Journal of Leadership Studies* 1, no. 2 (2006): 6–66.

Worrall, Di. *Accountability Leadership: How Great Leaders Build a High Performance Culture of Accountability and Responsibility*. Carlton, NSW, Australia: Di Worrall, 2013.

Zipkin, Nina. "8 Far-Out 'Jetsons' Contraptions That Actually Exist Today." *Entrepreneur*, April 17, 2015. https://www.entrepreneur.com/article/245192.

LEADERSHIP PASSPORT

If you have feedback or comments regarding this book or desire information about how to thrive in leadership and organizational culture, please go to www.leadershippassport.com or contact Leadership Passport by emailing thrive@leadershippassport.com.

Lightning Source UK Ltd.
Milton Keynes UK
UKHW052018010822
406702UK00004B/194